History Summarized
COLD WAR

WORLD
BOOK

www.worldbook.com

World Book, Inc.
180 North LaSalle Street
Suite 900
Chicago, Illinois 60601
USA

For information about other "History Summarized" titles, as well as other World Book print and digital publications, please go to **www.worldbook.com**.

For information about other World Book publications, call 1-800-WORLDBK (967-5325).

For information about sales to schools and libraries, call 1-800-975-3250 (United States) or 1-800-837-5365 (Canada).

Library of Congress Cataloging-in-Publication Data for this volume has been applied for.

History Summarized
ISBN: 978-0-7166-3800-1 (set, hc.)

Cold War
978-0-7166-3802-5 (hc.)

Also available as:
ISBN: 978-0-7166-3812-4 (e-book)

Printed in China by Shenzhen Wing King Tong Paper Products Co., Ltd., Shenzhen Guangdong
1st printing July 2018

STAFF

Writer: Tom Firme

Executive Committee

President
Jim O'Rourke

Vice President and
Editor in Chief
Paul A. Kobasa

Vice President, Finance
Donald D. Keller

Vice President, Marketing
Jean Lin

Vice President, International
Maksim Rutenberg

Vice President, Technology
Jason Dole

Director, Human Resources
Bev Ecker

Editorial

Director, New Print
Tom Evans

Manager
Jeff De La Rosa

Senior Editor
Shawn Brennan

Librarian
S. Thomas Richardson

Manager, Contracts and
Compliance
(Rights and Permissions)
Loranne K. Shields

Manager, Indexing Services
David Pofelski

Digital

Director, Digital Product
Development
Erika Meller

Digital Product Manager
Jonathan Wills

Manufacturing/Production

Manufacturing Manager
Anne Fritzinger

Production Specialist
Curley Hunter

Proofreader
Nathalie Strassheim

Graphics and Design

Senior Art Director
Tom Evans

Coordinator, Design
Development and Production
Brenda Tropinski

Senior Visual
Communications Designer
Melanie Bender

Senior Designer
Isaiah Sheppard

Media Editor
Rosalia Bledsoe

Senior Cartographer
John M. Rejba

TABLE OF CONTENTS

"History Summarized"

   Each book in this series concisely surveys a major historical event or interrelated series of events or a major cultural, economic, political or social movement. Especially important and interesting aspects of the subject of each book are highlighted in feature sections. Use a "History Summarized" book as an introduction to its subject in preparation for deeper study or as a review of the subject to reinforce what has been studied about the topic.

What was the Cold War?

The Cold War (1945-1991) describes the intense rivalry that developed after World War II (1939-1945) between groups of Communist and non-Communist nations. On one side were the Union of Soviet Socialist Republics (the Soviet Union) and its Communist allies, often referred to as the *Eastern bloc.* On the other side were the United States and its mostly democratic allies, usually referred to as the *Western bloc.* The struggle was called the *Cold War* because it did not actually lead to fighting, or "hot" war, on a wide scale. Still, between 1945 and 1991, millions of people died in the Cold War's "hot theaters"—that is, places where military action occurred—mainly in Africa, Asia, and Latin America.

The Cold War was characterized by mutual distrust, suspicion, and misunderstandings among the United States, the Soviet Union, and their allies. At times, these conditions increased the likelihood of a third world war. The United States accused the Soviet Union of seeking to expand Communism throughout the world. The Soviets, meanwhile, charged the United States with practicing imperialism and interfering with other countries. Each bloc's vision of the world contributed to East-West tension. The United States claimed to want a world of independent, democratic nations. On the other hand, the Soviet Union attempted to tightly control areas it considered vital to its national interest. Such areas included much of Eastern Europe.

Soldiers and sailors from many countries line up and march in formation during a parade outside the Allies Headquarters Building in the Russian port of Vladivostok in 1918.

CHAPTER ONE

The development of the Cold War

A lthough the Cold War (1945-1991) did not begin until the end of World War II (1939-1945), relations between the United States and the Soviet Union had been strained for decades. In 1917, a revolution in Russia established a Communist dictatorship there. From 1918 to 1920, the Communists and the anti-Communists in Russia fought a bloody civil war. Several other countries—including Canada, France, Japan, the United Kingdom, and the United States—sent troops to support the anti-Communists. Nevertheless, the Communists defeated their opponents. The Communist government created the Soviet Union in 1922.

During the 1920's and the 1930's, the Soviets called for world revolution. They hoped to destroy capitalism, which was the economic system of the United States. After a slight lessening of tensions, the United States granted diplomatic recognition to the Soviet Union in 1933.

In 1941, during World War II, Germany attacked the Soviet Union. The Soviet Union then joined the Western Allies in defeating Germany. For a time in 1945, it seemed possible that a lasting friendship might develop between the United States and the Soviet Union. However, major differences remained between the two, particularly about the status of the countries of Eastern Europe.

Two hostile blocs soon emerged. (A *bloc* is a group of nations combined for a purpose or having common interests.) The United States led the Western bloc. By the early 1950's, this group included Australia,

Canada, France, Japan, the United Kingdom, West Germany, and many other countries. The Soviet Union led the Eastern bloc, which included Albania, Bulgaria, Czechoslovakia, East Germany, Hungary, Poland, and Romania. China joined the Eastern bloc following the Communist takeover of its government in 1949. *Neutral* nations—those in neither bloc—included Cambodia, India, Indonesia, Yugoslavia, and many Middle Eastern and African nations.

During the late 1940's and the 1950's, Cold War tensions grew. Each side accused the other of wanting to rule the world. Each side believed its political and economic systems were better than the other's. They strengthened their armed forces. Both sides viewed the Cold War as a dispute between right and wrong. They saw every revolt and every international incident as part of the struggle. It was difficult to settle any dispute peacefully through compromise. Fear grew that a local conflict would touch off a third world war that might destroy humanity.

The nature of the Cold War began to change in the 1960's. Neither the East nor the West remained a *monolith* (united bloc). Communist China challenged Soviet leadership. France and West Germany often acted independently of U.S. policies. The Communist takeover of Cuba stirred anti-American feelings in Latin America. The rapid economic growth of China, Japan, and West Germany made them important nations in the struggle for power.

In 1970, Soviet and West German leaders signed a peace treaty. In 1971, China joined the United Nations (UN). In 1979, China and the United States established diplomatic relations.

Cold War tensions rose again in the late 1970's, peaking with the Soviet invasion of Afghanistan in 1979. In the following years, however, tensions eased after economic, political, and social reforms within the Soviet Union. Tensions relaxed further after the signing of a U.S.-Soviet

By the late 1940's, the Soviet Union had occupied East Germany and helped set up Communist governments in Poland, Czechoslovakia, Hungary, Romania, and Bulgaria. It also influenced Communist Yugoslavia and Albania. Communist rule ended in most of these countries in the late 1980's and early 1990's.

arms-control agreement and the withdrawal of Soviet troops from Afghanistan.

Beginning with the 1989 fall of the Berlin Wall, democratic reforms began in Eastern Europe. (The Berlin Wall was built in 1961 to divide the two parts of the city of Berlin—Communist East Berlin and non-Communist West Berlin. Berlin was in Communist East Germany, but the Western allies of West Germany controlled West Berlin.) In 1991, the Soviet Union broke up into a number of independent, non-Communist states. These reforms and other developments marked the end of the Cold War.

In August 1991, Communist officials attempted to overthrow Soviet leader Mikhail S. Gorbachev. More than 130,000 people filled Palace Square in Leningrad (now St. Petersburg) to demonstrate against the coup.

The coming of the Cold War

Historians do not agree on exactly when the Cold War began. But most agree that the Yalta Conference, a meeting of World War II Allied leaders in February 1945, marked the high point of wartime goodwill between the United States and the Soviet Union. Most historians also agree that relations between the two countries grew noticeably worse within the first year after the conference.

With Nazi Germany facing defeat in World War II, the leaders of the "Big Three" nations met at the Yalta Conference to plan for the peace that would follow the war. These leaders were President Franklin D. Roosevelt of the United States, Prime Minister Winston Churchill of the United Kingdom, and Premier Joseph Stalin of the Soviet Union. At Yalta, the leaders agreed to set up *occupation zones* (areas controlled by the Allies) for postwar Germany. They also made plans to form the United Nations. In addition, Stalin promised that the Soviets would go to war against Japan within three months after Germany surrendered.

Yalta Conference

The Yalta Conference was one of the most important meetings of key Allied leaders during World War II (1939-1945). These leaders were President Franklin D. Roosevelt (1882-1945) of the United States, Prime Minister Winston Churchill (1874-1965) of Britain, and Premier Joseph Stalin (1879-1953) of the Soviet Union. Their countries became known as the "Big Three." The conference took place at Yalta, a famous Black Sea resort on the Crimean Peninsula, from Feb. 4 to 11, 1945. Through the years, decisions made there regarding divisions in Europe have caused bitter debates.

When the meeting began, the Soviet Union held the strongest European military position. Soviet armies occupied much of Eastern Europe, and they were preparing to enter Berlin, Germany. The agenda at the Yalta Conference included addressing what the leaders thought would be the major problems in a postwar Europe.

Roosevelt, Churchill, and Stalin agreed on several points. These points were (1) to accept the structure of a world peacekeeping organization that was to become the United Nations; (2) to reestablish order in Europe and to help the defeated countries create democratic governments; (3) to divide Germany into four zones that would be occupied by Britain, the United States, the Soviet Union, and France; (4) to support the Soviet-backed government and hold free elections in Poland, and to extend the Soviet Union's territory into Poland; and (5) to force Germany to give the Soviet Union equipment and other resources to make up for Soviet losses. The Soviet Union also agreed to enter the war against Japan in exchange for control of the Kuril Islands, the southern half of Sakhalin Island, and two strategic ports.

The Yalta Conference was a meeting of the three key Allied leaders near the end of World War II. They were (left to right) Winston Churchill, prime minister of the United Kingdom; Franklin D. Roosevelt, president of the United States; and Joseph Stalin, premier of the Soviet Union.

After the war, critics said Roosevelt had "sold out" Eastern Europe and had given too much to the Soviet Union. But most modern scholars believe the conference produced a traditional and balanced settlement. They argue that the Soviet Union held the superior military and political position in Eastern Europe and yet made the greatest concessions at the conference. Stalin failed to win demands for huge sums of money from Germany to pay for tremendous war losses and for a shift of the German-Polish border westward. Most scholars also believe the Soviet Union's domination of Eastern Europe resulted from earlier and later events, not from decisions made at the Yalta Conference.

The Allied leaders also developed the Declaration on Liberated Europe, in which they pledged to hold democratic elections in countries freed from the control of Germany and its allies. However, the Soviet Union failed to keep this agreement. At the time it was made, Soviet forces had driven German troops out of most of Eastern Europe and had established a pro-Communist government in Poland. Despite the Declaration on Liberated Europe, Stalin was determined to maintain tight control over Eastern Europe. He especially felt that control of Poland, which had been used as a route to invade the Soviet Union, was necessary to Soviet security. The United States felt betrayed by Stalin's refusal to carry out his promises and by his determination to establish a "sphere of influence" in Eastern Europe.

Roosevelt died in April 1945, and Vice President Harry S. Truman (1884-1972) succeeded him as president. Germany surrendered in May. The main Allied leaders met for the final time at Potsdam, Germany, near Berlin, in July. Just before the meeting, the British Labour Party defeated Churchill's Conservative Party in an election. Clement R. Attlee succeeded Churchill as prime minister of the United Kingdom during the Potsdam Conference.

At Potsdam, the Allies agreed that the German people should be allowed to rebuild their lives "on a democratic and peaceful basis." However, serious disagreements arose. The United Kingdom and the United States charged that the Soviet Union was turning Eastern Europe to Communism. Even before World War II ended, the Soviet Union had taken over the Baltic nations of Estonia, Latvia, and Lithuania; parts of the countries of Finland, Poland, and Romania; and the eastern region of what then was Czechoslovakia. After the war, Soviet troops occupied a third of Germany and all of Bulgaria, Hungary, Poland, and Romania. Nevertheless, the Western nations reluctantly

The Potsdam Conference was the last meeting among the leaders of the Soviet Union, the United Kingdom, and the United States during World War II. It took place at Potsdam, Germany, near Berlin, from July 17 to Aug. 2, 1945, following Germany's defeat in the war.

agreed to transfer a large piece of German territory to Polish control.

The Iron Curtain descends

During 1945 and early 1946, the Soviet Union cut off nearly all contacts between the West and the occupied territories of Eastern Europe. In March 1946, Churchill warned that "an iron curtain has descended across the Continent" of Europe. He made popular the phrase *Iron Curtain* to refer to Soviet barriers against the West, particularly trade barriers and a rigid censorship that cut off the country and its Eastern European "satellite" countries from the rest of the world. Behind these barriers, the Soviet Union steadily expanded its power.

By 1945, Albania and what was then the country of Yugoslavia had become Communist. Italy began occupying Albania in 1939, but when

Women members of the Partisans in Yugoslavia train in 1944 at the Allied base in Italy, where they had been recuperating from injuries.

Italy surrendered to the Allies in 1943, German troops occupied Albania.

During World War II, there were three main resistance movements in Albania: (1) a nationalist movement called Balli Kombetar (*BAH lee KOM buh TAHR*), led by Midhat Frashëri (*miht HAHT FRAHSH uhr ee*); (2) a royalist group called the Legality Movement, headed by Abas Kupi (*ah BAHZ KOO pee*); and (3) a Communist organization called the National Liberation Front (NLF), led by Enver Hoxha (*HAW jah*). These groups fought against one another as well as against the German occupation forces.

In 1944, the Germans were driven out of Albania, and the Communists gained control of the country. Hoxha established a Communist government at Tiranë (*tee RAH nuh*) that year, and he began ruling the country as first secretary of the Communist Party. The Communists greatly restricted the people's freedom.

The Communist Party in Yugoslavia had helped the Communists of Albania organize the NLF, and relations with Albania remained close until 1948. But in that year, a split developed between the Soviet Union and Yugoslavia. The split resulted in the expulsion of Yugoslavia from the Cominform, a Soviet-dominated organization of European Communist parties. The people of Albania supported the Soviet Union to free themselves from Yugoslav influence. They also hoped to obtain Soviet aid in gaining control of a part of Yugoslavia where Albanians lived.

For Yugoslavia, this was a steady development during World War II. While German and other Axis troops occupied Yugoslavia, a resistance movement against Axis occupation spread among the Yugoslav people. Some of them joined the Partisans, a group led by Josip Broz Tito (*YOH seep brohz TEE toh*) and the Communist Party. Other Yugoslavs joined the Chetniks, a group headed by Draza Mihajlovic (*mee HY loh vihch*). The Partisans wanted to form a Communist government. The Chetniks supported the government of King Peter, who was in London orchestrating a government-in-exile.

The two resistance groups fought each other, as well as the occupation forces. At first, the Allies provided the Chetniks with weapons and supplies. But they switched their support to the Partisans in 1943 because Tito's forces were more effective against the Axis. The Partisans gained the support of the Yugoslav people. The Communists set up a temporary government in Jajce (*YEYE cheh*) (now in Bosnia-Herzegovina) in November 1943. Aided by Allied troops, the Partisans freed the Yugoslav capital, Belgrade, from occupation in 1944. The Communists then began to govern from the capital. By the time the European front of World War II ended in May 1945, Tito and the Communists controlled Yugoslavia.

On Nov. 29, 1945, Yugoslavia became a republic. It was called the Federal People's Republic of Yugoslavia. The monarchy was abolished. King Peter never returned to Yugoslavia. The 1946 Constitution organized Yugoslavia as a *federal* state. That meant that each of its republic largely controlled its own affairs. The six republics were Bosnia-Herzegovina, Croatia, Macedonia, Montenegro, Serbia, and Slovenia. Kosovo and Vojvodina (*VOY vuh dee nuh*) became autonomous regions (later autonomous provinces) of Serbia.

Only one political party, the Communist Party, was permitted. The

Josip Tito (left), the Communist leader of Yugoslavia, addresses a crowd from the Council of Ministers in Sofia, Bulgaria, in 1947.

government took control of farms, factories, and other businesses. The Communists began changing Yugoslavia from an agricultural country into an industrial one. Opponents of the Communist government were either imprisoned or exiled. Mihajlovic was executed in 1946. Roman Catholic Archbishop of Zagreb Alojzije Stepinac (*uh LOY zee yeh steh PEE nahts*) resisted the Communist takeover. He was imprisoned on false charges of having aided Germany and Italy during World War II.

In 1946, the Soviets organized Communist governments in Bulgaria and Romania. Under the protection of Soviet troops, Romanian Communists took over the government after World War II. They killed or imprisoned their political opponents and forced King Michael to give up his throne on Dec. 30, 1947.

The Communists declared Romania an "independent people's democracy." But Romania was a Soviet "satellite." In this context, *satellite* means a country that claims to be independent but is actually under the control of another country. In 1948 and 1952, Romania adopted constitutions that praised the Soviet Union. Romania's government, educational system, and other institutions were modeled on those of the Soviet Union. Soviet leaders directed Romania's economy and forced the country to emphasize agriculture and neglect industry. They also set the foreign policy of Romania.

On Sept. 8, 1944, the Soviet Union invaded Bulgaria, which was an Axis ally. The day after the Soviet invasion, the Fatherland Front, a group of Bulgarian political organizations led by the Communist Party, overthrew the Bulgarian government.

The Communists did not completely control Bulgaria's new government, and so they immediately took steps to strengthen their power. They removed non-Communists from the government. People whom they considered to be enemies were killed or sent to labor camps or prisons. Private property was seized, and the citizens' freedoms were restricted. In 1946, the monarchy was abolished. Georgi Dimitrov, the chief Communist leader, became head of government. In 1947, Bulgaria adopted a constitution modeled on that of the Soviet Union. By 1948, the Communists had total control of the country.

In 1947, Communists took control of Hungary and Poland. After the German attack against the Soviet Union in 1941, Polish Communists formed an exile center in the Soviet Union. Poles, under the command of the Soviet Union, fought against Germany on the eastern front. The Communists also formed their own small underground movement. In 1942, they established the Polish Communist Party. Wladyslaw Gomulka (*vlah DIH slahf guh MOO kah*) became the party leader in 1943.

In 1944, the Soviet Union's army invaded Poland and began driving out the Germans. Also in 1944, the Home Army staged an uprising against the Germans in Warsaw. But after two months of fighting, the Home Army had to surrender. That same year, a Polish Committee of National Liberation was formed in Lublin. The Soviet Union recognized the committee, which consisted almost entirely of Communists, as the provisional government of Poland. At the 1945 Yalta Conference, the Allies agreed to recognize the committee after it was expanded to include representatives of the London government-in-exile and other non-Communist groups.

Agreements reached at the end of the war shifted Poland's borders westward, and millions of Poles were resettled. The Soviet Union kept most of eastern Poland. In return, Poland received the German lands east of the Oder (*OH duhr*) and Neisse (*NY suh*) rivers, including major industrial regions.

Communist rule was opposed by most Poles. But the Communists used police power and other methods to crush resistance. Communist-

Communist-controlled elections in Poland in 1947 gave the party a large majority in the new legislature.

controlled elections in 1947 gave them a large majority in the new legislature. By 1948, Communist rule was firmly established.

The Soviet Union invaded Hungary late in 1944, and Hungary and the Allies signed an armistice in January 1945. Hungary agreed to give up all the territory it had gained since 1938. Hungary and the Allies signed a peace treaty in 1947.

Elections were held in November 1945, a year after Soviet troops invaded. Early the next year, Hungary was declared a republic. After the November elections, a coalition government was formed. This government introduced many social and economic reforms, including land

The Soviet Union covered more than half of Europe and nearly two-fifths of Asia. This map shows the country's 15 republics and the dates when they became republics. The Soviet Union dissolved in 1991. The republics are now independent nations.

distribution among the peasants. The coalition consisted of the Smallholder, Social Democratic, Communist, and National Peasant parties. The Smallholder Party had won a clear majority of the votes in the elections. However, Communists gradually gained control of the government, largely because of the continued presence of Soviet troops in Hungary.

Elections were held again in 1947, and the Communists again failed to win a majority of the votes. But by then, Communist Party leaders held important positions at all levels of government and in major nongovernmental organizations. Only a small percentage of Hungary's people belonged to the party. However, Communist Party members held enough key government posts to extend their control over the country. The general secretary, head of the Communist Party, became the most power-ful leader in Hungary.

The Communist leaders made the Communist Party the country's only legal political party, and they banned all opposition parties. In 1949, the Communists gave Hungary a constitution patterned on that of the Soviet Union.

Communists seized full power in Czechoslovakia early in 1948 as they caused a crisis that led to the resignation of non-Communist government ministers and created a government dominated by Communists. This came two years after the government put many of the country's major industries under state control, forced hundreds of thousands of Germans and Hungarians living in Czechoslovakia to leave, and had an election in which the Communist Party won the most votes, with Communist Party Chairman Klement Gottwald becoming prime minister. Gottwald became president in 1948. Czechoslovakia's Communist leaders copied the Soviet model of political organization and economic development. The Commu-nist Party became the only powerful political party. The government managed all aspects of the economy. Farmers were forced to join either state farms or *collectives*. The government owned and operated state farms. On collective farms, farmworkers jointly owned the farm equip-ment and property.

Albania, Yugoslavia, Bulgaria, Romania, Hungary, and Poland became Soviet satellites. Loyalty to the Soviet Union varied between satellite countries. The Soviets tightly controlled domestic affairs with each satel-lite.

While the Soviet Union spread its influence to its satellites and other countries, it confronted the U.S. on different fronts. The U.S. attempted to contain the spread of communism and was successful in some cases. Also, the Soviet Union and the United States would engage in an arms race.

On April 4, 1949, the United States, Canada, the United Kingdom, France, and eight other nations signed the North Atlantic Treaty. The 12 nations thus formed the North Atlantic Treaty Organization (NATO).

CHAPTER TWO

The West holds the line

In the fall of 1946, Greek Communists revolted against the Greek government. The United Kingdom had given military and economic aid to Greece. However, the British told the United States they could no longer give the Greeks enough help. The British also warned that they could not help Turkey resist Communist pressure.

In March 1947, President Truman declared that the United States would help any free nation resist Communist *aggression* (attack). Congress granted his request for $400 million to aid Greece and Turkey. With this aid, both Greece and Turkey successfully resisted Communism. The new American policy became known as the Truman Doctrine. Aimed at Soviet expansion in Europe and the Middle East, the Truman Doctrine developed into the *containment policy.* The containment policy was designed to *contain* (hold back) the expansion of Communism throughout the world.

American diplomat George Frost Kennan (1904-2005) was credited with developing the containment policy. Kennan was a major architect of the Marshall Plan for post-World War II reconstruction of Europe. He served on the U.S. Department of State policy-planning staff in 1947. As ambassador to the Soviet Union in 1952, Kennan protested being restricted to Moscow. The Soviets demanded his dismissal. Later, he was ambassador to Yugoslavia from 1961 to 1963. The foreign ministers of France, the Soviet Union, the United Kingdom, and the United States met in Moscow in March and April 1947. They tried to draw up a German peace treaty. But the ministers could not agree on ways to end the occupation or on how to unify Germany.

The failure of the conference convinced U.S. Secretary of State George C. Marshall (1880-1959) that the Soviet Union would not help Europe recover from World War II. In June 1947, Marshall proposed giving U.S. economic aid to all European nations that would cooperate in plans for their own recovery. This proposal grew into the European Recovery Program, or Marshall Plan, which began in 1948. The United States believed that a strong, stable Western Europe would block the spread of Communism. Meanwhile, in September 1947, Stalin and other Communist party leaders set up the Cominform (Communist Information Bureau), a Soviet-dominated organization of Communist parties in Europe.

Czechoslovakia and Poland wanted to take part in the Marshall Plan, but the Soviet Union would not let them accept U.S. aid. Instead, the Soviets set up the Council for Mutual Economic Assistance (COMECON) in January 1949. This organization was designed to unite the East European satellites economically and politically.

In June 1948, the Western Allies announced plans to unify their German occupation zones and establish the West German Federal Republic (West Germany). West Germany was formally established in September 1949. It had independence in some of its internal affairs, and it joined the Marshall Plan.

Also in June 1948, the Soviet Union harshly criticized Josip Tito, the Communist leader of Yugoslavia. Tito then began to develop his own style of Communism for Yugoslavia, free from Soviet control. That year, Stalin broke off relations with Yugoslavia. The Cominform expelled Yugoslavia's party and withdrew all aid. Yugoslavia turned to the United States and other Western countries for help. In 1951, the United States began providing Yugoslavia with economic aid. Later, the United States

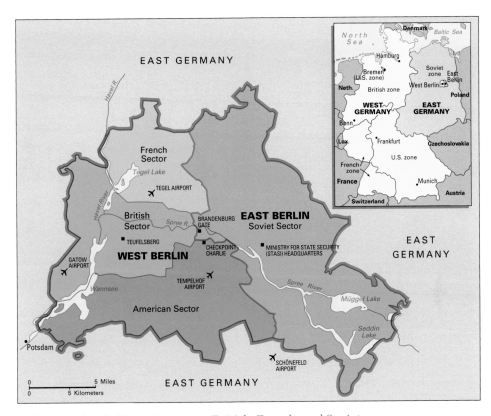

EAST GERMANY

French
Sector

Tegel Lake

✈ TEGEL AIRPORT

Havel R.

Havel River

British
Sector

Spree R.

BRANDENBURG
GATE

EAST BERLIN
Soviet Sector

■ TEUFELSBERG

WEST BERLIN

■ CHECKPOINT
CHARLIE

■ MINISTRY FOR STATE SECURITY
(STASI) HEADQUARTERS

GATOW
AIRPORT ✈

Wannsee

TEMPELHOF ✈
AIRPORT

Spree River

American Sector

Müggel Lake

*Seddin
Lake*

✈Potsdam

✈ SCHÖNEFELD
AIRPORT

EAST
GERMANY

EAST GERMANY

0 ____ 5 Miles
0 ____ 5 Kilometers

North
Sea

Denmark *Baltic Sea*

•Hamburg

Bremen•
(U.S. zone)

Soviet
zone East
Berlin

Neth.

British zone

West Berlin

Poland

**WEST
GERMANY**

**EAST
GERMANY**

Bonn•

Lux.

•Frankfurt

Czechoslovakia

U.S. zone

French
zone

France

•Munich

Austria

Switzerland

Berlin was divided into American, British, French, and Soviet
sectors (districts) after World War II ended in 1945. The
American, British, and French sectors became known as West
Berlin. The Soviet sector became known as East Berlin.

also granted military assistance.

After the split with the Soviet Union, Yugoslavia began to develop its
own style of Communist government. In 1955, two years after Stalin's
death, Soviet and Yugoslav leaders reopened relations. But Tito refused
to take sides in the political rivalry between Communist countries and
Western democracies. Instead, he became a leading spokesman for
uncommitted countries.

Josip Broz Tito

Josip Broz Tito (*YOH seep brohz TEE toh*) (1892-1980) established a Communist government in Yugoslavia after World War II and then became the country's ruler. He led Yugoslavia in its separation from control by the Soviet Union. His actions set an example that China and some Eastern European Communist nations later followed. Tito was the first Communist leader to permit his people some economic and social freedom.

Tito was born Josip Broz, the son of a peasant family, in Kumrovec, Croatia, on May 7, 1892. At that time, Croatia was part of the empire of Austria-Hungary. Broz became a metalworker. He was drafted into the Austro-Hungarian Army in 1913. In 1915, during World War I (1914-1918), he was wounded and captured by Russian troops. In 1917, the Communists released him from prison after they had taken power in Russia. Broz joined the Communist Party.

In 1920, Broz returned to his homeland, which had become part of the new Kingdom of the Serbs, Croats, and Slovenes (later renamed Yugoslavia). He helped organize the Yugoslav Communist Party. But it was outlawed, and Broz was sent to jail in 1928.

He used the name *Tito* to confuse the police after his release in 1934. He later added *Tito* to his real name. He was secretary-general to the Yugoslav Communist Party from 1937 until 1966, when he became party president.

During World War II, Tito organized and led the *Partisans,* guerrillas who fought Germans occupying Yugoslavia. Another resistance group, the anti-Communist *Chetniks,* fought the Partisans, but lost. After the war, Tito had Chetnik leader Draza Mihajlovic executed.

Tito set up a Communist government in Yugoslavia in 1945, and it was recognized by the United Kingdom, the United States, and the Soviet Union. Tito became prime minister and defense minister. But Soviet efforts to control Yugoslavia led to a split between Tito and Soviet dictator Joseph Stalin, who expelled Yugoslavia from the Soviet bloc in 1948. Tito became the first independent Communist leader. Later, he became a spokesman for nations that refused to take sides in the Cold War.

But Tito kept tight control over the Yugoslav people and tolerated no opposition. In 1963, Tito made himself president for life. Later, Tito limited the power of the secret police and encouraged some economic and political freedom. In 1968, Tito supported Czechoslovakia's liberalization program, and he criticized the Soviet Union for sending troops into the country to stop the reforms. In 1971, he became head of a presidential council formed to rule Yugoslavia. As chairman, Tito retained much of his power until his death on May 4, 1980.

From June 1948 to September 1949, the Berlin Airlift supplied West Berlin with food and fuel entirely by airplanes. The airlift delivered food, coal, petroleum, and other supplies to more than 2 million people in West Berlin.

The Berlin blockade

The Berlin blockade was the Soviet answer to the West's plans for West Germany. In June 1948, Soviet troops blocked all railroad, highway, and water traffic through East Germany to West Berlin. The city lay 110 miles (177 kilometers) inside the Soviet occupation zone. The Western powers generally brought supplies to West Berlin by trucks or railroad

cars. Soviet leaders thought their blockade would force the West to leave Berlin. Instead of pulling out of West Berlin, the Americans, British, and French set up the Berlin Airlift. From June 1948 to September 1949, they supplied West Berlin with food and fuel entirely by airplanes. The airlift delivered food, coal, petroleum, and other supplies to more than 2 million people in West Berlin. In more than 250,000 flights, the planes flew in more than 2 million tons (1.8 million metric tons) of goods. The Berlin Airlift, which saved West Berliners from starvation, ranks among the most important and dramatic incidents of the early Cold War. The Soviets lifted their blockade in May 1949.

NATO

Military strength became more and more important in the late 1940's. During the Berlin blockade, the United States pledged continuing military aid to Western Europe. The United States, Canada, and 10 Western European nations signed the North Atlantic Treaty in April 1949. This mutual defense treaty set up the North Atlantic Treaty Organization (NATO), a military alliance. The goals of the alliance included the prevention of Soviet expansion and the defense of West Germany. In September 1951, the United States signed the ANZUS mutual defense treaty with Australia and New Zealand.

NATO consisted of the United States, the United Kingdom, Canada, and more than 20 other member countries. NATO seeks to protect the freedom and security of its member countries through political and military efforts. The organization also participates in a variety of international peacekeeping and crisis management efforts.

Originally, the central purpose of NATO was to discourage an attack by the Soviet Union on the non-Communist nations of Western Europe. By joining NATO, each member country agreed to treat an attack on any other member as an attack on itself. NATO's collective defense policy was known as *deterrence* because it was designed to *deter* (discourage) a Soviet attack.

In 1955, the Soviet Union and its allies formed their own military alliance, called the Warsaw Pact, to oppose NATO. Albania, Bulgaria, Czechoslovakia, East Germany, Hungary, Poland, Romania, and the

At a ceremony in the Oval Office of the White House, in Washington,
D.C., on Aug. 24, 1949, U.S. President Harry Truman (seated) formally
accepted the instruments of ratification and announced that the North
Atlantic Treaty was in effect. The United States, Canada, and 10
Western European nations signed the treaty in April 1949.

Soviet Union signed the treaty in Warsaw that May. They claimed they
signed the Warsaw Pact as a response to the creation of NATO. Albania
withdrew from the Warsaw Pact in 1968.

Since the end of the Cold War in the early 1990's, the main focus of
NATO has shifted toward general crisis management and peacekeeping.
Today, the organization's central aims include resolving international
conflicts and crises, developing and enforcing international security
policies, fighting terrorism, and working to maintain peace and stability.

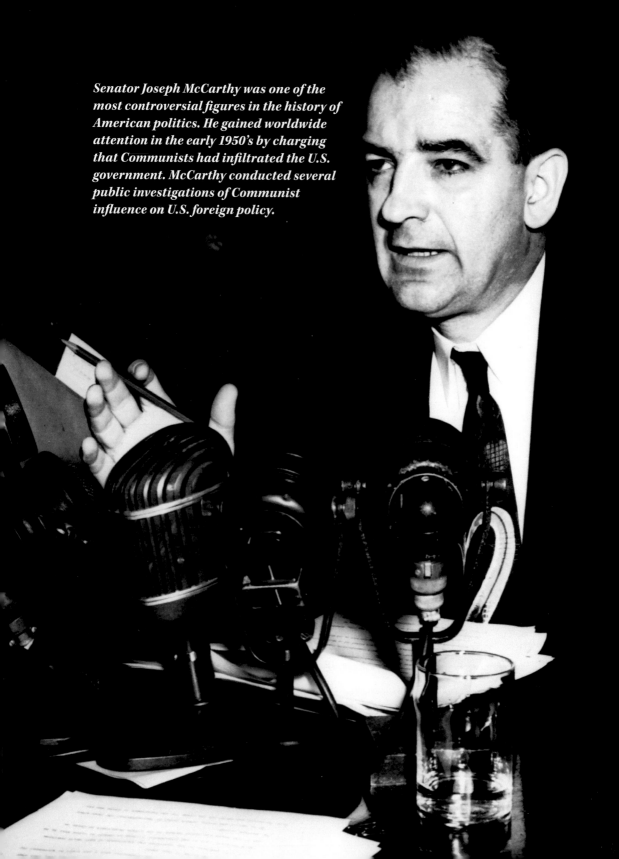

Senator Joseph McCarthy was one of the most controversial figures in the history of American politics. He gained worldwide attention in the early 1950's by charging that Communists had infiltrated the U.S. government. McCarthy conducted several public investigations of Communist influence on U.S. foreign policy.

CHAPTER THREE

Blacklisting and McCarthyism

T he Un-American Activities Committee was an investigating committee of the United States House of Representatives. It investigated the threat of *subversion* (overthrowing the government) by groups in the United States and recommended legislation to the House.

The House Committee on Un-American Activities (HUAC) grew from a special investigating committee established in 1938. It became a *standing* (permanent) committee in 1945. The committee's main interest was to search for Communist influence inside and outside the government. After World War II ended in 1945, many people viewed such investigations as a contribution to the struggle against world Communism. U.S. President Harry S. Truman established a loyalty-security program in 1947 after it was discovered that some Communists had held jobs within the government before and during the war. The committee also investigated the activities of other radical or extremist groups.

The committee received attention in 1947 for its hearings on the influence of Communism in the motion-picture industry. But it gained its greatest attention in 1948 during its investigation of Communists in the Department of State. Its hearings led to the perjury trial and conviction of Alger Hiss, a former high official of the department. Representative Richard M. Nixon (1913-1994), a committee member and future U.S. president, played a key role in the investigation. (A person commits *perjury* by claiming something is true that the person knows to be false.)

The Hollywood blacklist

The Hollywood blacklist was a term used to describe a policy carried out in the mid-1900's by major entertainment companies in the United States against American entertainment professionals who were suspected of being Communists or Communist sympathizers. Many American actors, directors, screenwriters, radio commentators, musicians, and other people in the entertainment industry lost their jobs or were denied employment in the United States as a result of the blacklist.

Hollywood developed the blacklist in response to pressure from the House Committee on Un-American Activities (HUAC). Studio executives cooperated with the committee out of fear of government regulation, public disapproval, and box-office losses. The entertainment industry also created the blacklist as a show of Hollywood's patriotism during the Cold War.

In 1947, HUAC held hearings on the influence of Communism in the motion-picture industry. The committee summoned a number of people working in the industry to appear before it. Some called to testify gave the names of suspected Communists or Communist sympathizers. Some leading Hollywood figures organized the Committee for the First Amendment to protest HUAC's actions.

Ten writers and directors summoned by the committee refused to testify. They cited their First Amendment rights to freedom of speech and assembly. For their refusal to cooperate, they were found to be in contempt of Congress. A group of Hollywood studio executives announced that the 10 would be fired or suspended without pay. The blacklisted group came to be known as the Hollywood Ten. They all served one-year prison terms. The 10 were Alvah Bessie (1904-1985), a screenwriter, Herbert Biberman (1900-1971), a screenwriter and

Nine of the members of the Hollywood 10 were charged with contempt of Congress for refusing to testify before HUAC in 1947. They were (left to right) Adrian Scott, Edward Dmytryk, Samuel Ornitz, Lester Cole, Herbert Biberman, Albert Maltz, Alvah Bessie, John Howard Lawson, and Ring Lardner, Jr.

director, Lester Cole (1904-1985), a screenwriter, Edward Dmytryk (1908-1999), a director, Ring Lardner, Jr. (1915-2000), a screenwriter, John Howard Lawson (1894-1977), a screenwriter, Albert Maltz (1908-1985), a screenwriter, Samuel Ornitz (1890-1957), a screenwriter, Adrian Scott (1911-1972), a producer and screenwriter, and Dalton Trumbo (1905-1976), a screenwriter and novelist.

In 1951, HUAC launched a second investigation of Hollywood and Communism. Eventually, the studios blacklisted more than 300 people in the American entertainment industry, often with no evidence supporting the charges. Some of the blacklisted individuals left the United States to find work elsewhere, or they left the entertainment business. Some writers wrote under pseudonyms or the names of colleagues.

The second HUAC investigation ended in 1952, though some later investigations took place. But blacklisted film professionals were not eligible for Academy Award consideration until 1959. The blacklist effectively came to an end in 1960. That year, Universal Pictures gave Trumbo screen credit for his role as screenwriter on the motion picture *Spartacus.* However, most of those blacklisted were unable to work again in their profession for many years.

After the Hiss case, the Un-American Activities Committee looked into suspected Communist influence in almost all areas of life. Committees in the U.S. Senate and in state legislatures also investigated Communist influence. As a result, public employees and a number of employees in private industries were required to take loyalty oaths. Persons accused of Communist associations were *blacklisted* (denied employment) by some firms.

Many people believed the committee performed a valuable service by helping protect the United States from Communism. Critics, however, charged that the committee often abused its investigative power and violated the constitutional rights of witnesses. Some critics felt that people labeled as subversives should have the right to cross-examine their accusers. Others believed that the discovery of conspirators should be the responsibility of the police, the Federal Bureau of Investigation, and the courts. Decisions by the Supreme Court of the United States in the 1950's and 1960's curbed the committee's activities. For example, the court ruled that witnesses may refuse to answer any questions unrelated to the matter under investigation. In 1969, the House changed the committee's name to the Committee on Internal Security. The House abolished the committee in 1975.

McCarthyism

Joseph Raymond McCarthy (1908-1957), a Republican U.S. senator from Wisconsin, was one of the most controversial figures in American politics. He gained worldwide attention in the early 1950's by charging that Communists had infiltrated the government. McCarthy conducted several public investigations of Communist influence on U.S. foreign policy. Some people praised him as a patriot, but others condemned him for publicly accusing people of disloyalty without sufficient evidence. He failed to identify any Communists employed by the government.

McCarthy was elected to the Senate in 1946. The following year, President Truman established his loyalty boards to investigate federal workers and the U.S. attorney general established a list of organizations that the Department of Justice considered disloyal. Government agencies used the list as a guide to help determine the loyalty of employees and people seeking jobs.

McCarthy attracted national attention in 1950 by accusing the Department of State of harboring Communists. President Truman, a Democrat, and Secretary of State Dean Acheson (1893-1971) denied McCarthy's charges. The Senate Foreign Relations Committee investigated the department but found no Communists or Communist sympathizers there. Nevertheless, McCarthy made numerous additional accusations and gained many followers. He and other conservatives blamed many of the nation's problems on the supposed secret presence of Communists in the government.

Most of McCarthy's fellow senators of both parties were aware of his widespread support and were anxious to avoid challenging him. So was General Dwight D. Eisenhower (1890-1969), both as Republican presidential candidate and soon after becoming president in 1953. McCarthy also accused the Eisenhower Administration of treason.

The accusations and investigations spread quickly and affected thousands of people. Librarians, college professors, entertainers, journalists, clergy, and others came under suspicion.

Several circumstances caused many Americans to believe McCarthy's charges. These included the frustrations of the Korean War (1950-1953), the Chinese Communist conquest of mainland China, and the conviction of several Americans as Soviet spies. Charges that Americans had served as Soviet spies received wide attention. In addition to the convic-

Alger Hiss

Alger Hiss (1904-1996) became the center of a national controversy over Communist infiltration in the United States government during the administration of President Harry S. Truman in the 1940's and 1950's. A number of Republican congressmen, including Representative Richard M. Nixon, had charged the government with employing Communists who acted as secret agents for the Soviet Union.

The controversy reached a climax in 1948. Whittaker Chambers, a confessed former Communist spy, accused Hiss, a former high official in the U.S. Department of State, of having given him secret government documents in the 1930's. Hiss denied the charge but resigned from his position as head of the Carnegie Endowment for International Peace. Chambers produced microfilms of confidential government papers that he had hidden in a pumpkin on his farm in Maryland. He said Hiss had given him the secrets to send to the Soviet Union.

Hiss was brought to trial in 1949. He was charged with perjury for denying accusations that he gave away secret documents and for claiming that he had not seen Chambers since Jan. 1, 1937. By law, Hiss could not be charged for spying because too much time had passed. Important government officials, including two associate justices of the Supreme Court of the United States, testified for Hiss. But the jury could not agree on a verdict.

Hiss was brought to trial on the same perjury charges late in 1949. The government introduced new evidence in an attempt to prove that Hiss's personal typewriter had been used to copy 42 confidential government documents. On Jan. 21, 1950, the jury

Alger Hiss was accused of being a Soviet spy, He was brought to trial in 1949. Hiss was convicted of perjury largely on evidence supplied to the government by a confessed former Communist spy.

found him guilty. Hiss was sentenced to five years in prison. He was paroled after serving 3 years and 8 months, and he continued to declare his innocence.

Hiss was born on Nov. 11, 1904, in Baltimore and graduated from Johns Hopkins University and Harvard Law School. He served in the Department of State from 1935 to 1947. He participated in the Dumbarton Oaks Conference and the Yalta Conference. He served as secretary-general of the United Nations founding convention. He died on Nov. 15, 1996.

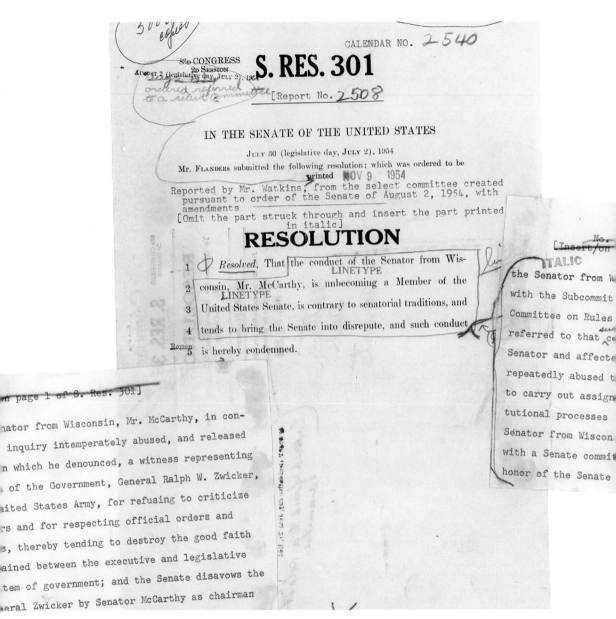

83D CONGRESS
2D SESSION

S. RES. 301

[Report No. 2508]

IN THE SENATE OF THE UNITED STATES

JULY 30 (legislative day, JULY 2), 1954

Mr. FLANDERS submitted the following resolution; which was ordered to be printed **NOV 9 1954**

Reported by Mr. Watkins, from the select committee created pursuant to order of the Senate of August 2, 1954, with amendments
[Omit the part struck through and insert the part printed in italic]

RESOLUTION

1 *Resolved*, That the conduct of the Senator from Wis-
LINETYPE
2 consin, Mr. McCarthy, is unbecoming a Member of the
LINETYPE
3 United States Senate, is contrary to senatorial traditions, and
4 tends to bring the Senate into disrepute, and such conduct
Roman
5 is hereby condemned.

[Insert on

ITALIC

the Senator from W

with the Subcommitt

Committee on Rules

referred to that c

Senator and affecte

repeatedly abused t

to carry out assign

tutional processes

Senator from Wiscon

with a Senate commit

honor of the Senate

n page 1 of S. Res. 301]

ator from Wisconsin, Mr. McCarthy, in con-

inquiry intemperately abused, and released

n which he denounced, a witness representing

of the Government, General Ralph W. Zwicker,

ited States Army, for refusing to criticize

s and for respecting official orders and

, thereby tending to destroy the good faith

ained between the executive and legislative

tem of government; and the Senate disavows the

eral Zwicker by Senator McCarthy as chairman

In Resolution 301, shown here, the Senate condemned McCarthy in 1954 for "contemptuous" conduct toward a subcommittee that had investigated his finances in 1952, and for his abuse of a committee that recommended he be censured.

tion and imprisonment of Hiss, the American couple Julius (1918-1953) and Ethel (1915-1953) Rosenberg were convicted of passing military secrets to Soviet agents in the 1940's and were executed.

During nationally televised hearings in 1954, McCarthy accused the U.S. Army of "coddling Communists." The Army made countercharges of improper conduct by members of McCarthy's staff. As a result of the hearings, McCarthy lost the support of millions of people. The Senate condemned him in 1954 for "contemptuous" conduct toward a subcommittee that had investigated his finances in 1952, and for his abuse of a committee that recommended he be censured.

From 1955 to 1958, the Supreme Court of the United States made a series of decisions that helped protect the rights of people accused of sympathizing with Communists. Today, the term *McCarthyism* is sometimes used to refer to reckless public accusations of disloyalty to the United States, as well as a broad term to describe specious witch hunts of various kinds.

McCarthy was born in Grand Chute, Wisconsin, on Nov. 14, 1908, and graduated from Marquette University. He wrote *America's Retreat from Victory: The Story of George Catlett Marshall* (1951) and *McCarthyism: The Fight for America* (1952). He died on May 2, 1957.

A vast column of radioactive water is thrown into the air by an undersea nuclear explosion in this 1946 photograph. The silhouettes of abandoned battleships can be seen against the ocean and sky. This nuclear weapons test, code-named Operation Crossroads, was one of more than 1,000 test explosions conducted by the United States.

CHAPTER FOUR

Nuclear arms race; Cold War in Asia

The nuclear arms race began on Aug. 29, 1949, when the Soviet Union tested an atomic bomb. Until then, the United States had been the only nation that knew how to make an atomic bomb. During the 1940's, Communist strength increased in Asia. The Soviet Red Army occupied Manchuria, a region in northeastern China, just before the end of World War II. After the army left in 1946, Chinese Communists took over most of northern Manchuria. The Soviets also set up a North Korean "people's republic."

In 1945, the United States sent General George C. Marshall to China to attempt to arrange a political settlement between the Nationalists and the Communists. However, neither the Nationalists, led by Chiang Kai-shek (*jyahng ky SHEHK*) (1887-1975), nor the Communists, led by Mao Zedong (*mow zeh dawng*) (1893-1976), believed that they could achieve their goals by coming to terms with the other side. In mid-1946, full-scale fighting between the Communists and Nationalists began.

The United States gave military aid to Chiang. Late in 1949, Chiang and his government fled to the island of Taiwan, near the mainland of China. The conquest of China by Mao's forces put China into the Communist bloc.

The beginning of Communist rule took place under the direction of Mao, the chairman of the Communist Party. Premier Zhou Enlai (*joh ehn ly*) (1898-1976) directed all government departments and ministries.

Military, technical, and economic help from the Soviet Union helped support the new government. From 1949 to 1952, the new government firmly established its control over China and worked to help the nation's economy recover.

The Korean War

At the end of World War II, Soviet troops occupied North Korea and U.S. forces occupied South Korea. The North Koreans had a strong army, receiving Soviet military aid even after Soviet troops withdrew late in 1948. The United States withdrew from South Korea in June 1949.

The Korean War began with the North Korean invasion of South Korea on June 25, 1950. On June 27, President Truman sent U.S. forces to aid South Korea. At the request of the United States, the United Nations Security Council voted to send UN troops to help South Korea. The Soviet delegation was *boycotting* (not attending) the council and missed a chance to veto the decision. Sixteen UN member nations sent troops to help South Korea. Chinese Communist troops aided North Korea.

Peace talks began in July 1951. They went on for two years while bloody fighting continued. Finally, in July 1953, representatives of the UN and the Communists signed an *armistice* (temporary peace). In 1954, representatives of both sides met in Geneva, Switzerland, to discuss a political settlement. However, they could not agree on a way to unite North and South Korea. Today, Korea remains divided.

The Korean War was the first war in which troops of a world organization fought an aggressor nation. It also marked the first time Americans fought a "hot war" against Communism. The Korean War extended the American containment policy to Asia. It also introduced *limited warfare* as a substitute to all-out—and possibly nuclear—war. Each side avoided attacking targets that could lead to expansion of the war. And each side

The Korean War (1950-1953) was the first war in which a world
organization, the United Nations (UN), played a military role. After
North Korean soldiers invaded South Korea in 1950, the UN asked
its member nations to supply South Korea with military aid. The
United States provided about 90 percent of the troops, supplies,
and other equipment that went to South Korea. In this photograph,
American soldiers take cover from incoming fire.

limited the weapons it used and the territory in which it would fight.

The death of Stalin

The Soviet leader Joseph Stalin died in March 1953, two months after
Dwight D. Eisenhower became president of the United States. Stalin's
death changed the character of the Cold War.

The new Soviet rulers governed as a committee at first. Premier Georgi
M. Malenkov (*gay AWR gih MAH luhn kawf*) (1902-1988) and his associ-
ates adopted a softer policy toward the Soviet satellites and the West.
For example, they allowed the Soviet wives of U.S. servicemen to follow

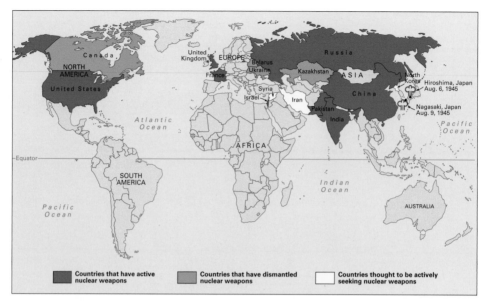

This map shows the status of nuclear weapons development throughout the world and the locations of the only two nuclear bombs ever used during warfare.

their husbands to America. The Soviets also set up a cultural exchange program with the West. Soviet troops put down a revolt in East Germany in June 1953, but the Soviet Union took a softer course of action on other issues.

The arms race continued. The United States tested its first hydrogen bomb, or H-bomb, in November 1952, and the Soviet Union set off its first H-bomb in November 1955. Military alliances strengthened during this period. West Germany joined NATO in 1955. In response, the Soviets and their Eastern European satellites signed the Warsaw Mutual Defense Pact, a military alliance. In 1955, the United States announced its support of the Baghdad Pact. The pact, later called the Central Treaty Organization, was a military alliance of Iran, Iraq, Pakistan, Turkey, and the United Kingdom that lasted until 1979.

In January 1954, the new U.S. secretary of state, John Foster Dulles

(*DUHL uhs*) (1888-1959), had outlined a new American military policy. The United States, he warned, would meet Communist aggression by "massive retaliation" with nuclear weapons. The United States, Dulles said, would strike back "at places and with means of our own choosing."

Cold War tensions increased in eastern Asia during 1954 and 1955. The nationalist Vietnamese in Indochina were led by Communists and supported by China. (*Indochina* is the eastern half of a long and curving peninsula that extends into the South China Sea from the mainland of Southeast Asia. Indochina comprises the three nations of Cambodia, Laos, and Vietnam.) In the spring of 1954, after years of fighting, they defeated the French at Dien Bien Phu (*dyehn byehn FOO*). The two sides signed a cease-fire agreement in Geneva in July 1954. It recognized the tempo-rary division of Viet-nam and gave North Vietnam to the Com-munists. Nationwide elections were to be

In 1954, Australia, New Zealand, the United Kingdom, the United States, and four other nations formed an alliance called the Southeast Asia Treaty Organization (SEATO). The group is shown at a 1955 council meeting in the throne room of Ananda Samkom Palace in Thailand.

held in 1956. However, neither the United States nor South Vietnam signed the agreement, and South Vietnam refused to hold the elections. The agreement also established the independence of Cambodia, Laos, and South Vietnam.

In 1954, Australia, New Zealand, the United Kingdom, the United States, and four other nations formed an alliance called the Southeast Asia Treaty Organization (SEATO). SEATO lasted until 1977. Its goal was to prevent further Communist expansion in Southeast Asia. After the defeat of France in Indochina, the United States increased its aid to South Vietnam. The United States believed that if one Southeast Asian nation fell to Communism, the others would also topple over, one after another. This belief was called the "domino theory." But even with U.S. support, South Vietnam could not defeat the Communist rebels. The rebels, called Viet Cong, were supported by North Vietnam. In 1955, the United States began sending military advisers to help the South Vietnamese government.

The United States also increased its support of the Chinese Nationalists on Taiwan. In September 1954, the Chinese Communists staged air and artillery attacks against the islands of Quemoy (*kih MOY*) and Matsu (*MAT soo*). These islands, in the Formosa Strait (now called the Taiwan Strait), were held by the Nationalist Chinese. In 1955, Congress voted to let President Eisenhower use armed force if necessary to protect the Chinese Nationalists.

The spirit of Geneva

In Europe, a "thaw" in the Cold War began in 1955. The Western Allies and the Soviet Union signed a peace treaty with Austria in May. Red Army troops left that country, and Austria became an independent, neutral nation. That same month, Nikita Sergeyevich Khrushchev (*nih*

KEE tuh surh GAY uh vihch KROOSH chehf), the Soviet Communist Party chief, apologized to Josip Tito and resumed trade with Yugoslavia.

Eisenhower and Khrushchev met in Geneva in July. Both leaders agreed that a nuclear war would be a disaster for both sides. Political observers began to write of a "big thaw" in East-West relations and called it the "spirit of Geneva." After the Geneva conference, the Soviet Union announced a reduction in its armed forces and its satellites' armies.

Also, during the Geneva conference, Eisenhower proposed an arrangement called Open Skies, under which the United States and the Soviet Union would allow air inspection of each other's military bases. But the Soviets rejected his proposal.

A long line of Soviet missiles parades into Moscow's Red Square in 1963. The military rivalry between the United States and the Soviet Union led many people to fear a third world war.

Nikita Sergeyevich Khrushchev

Nikita Sergeyevich Khrushchev (*nih KEE tuh surh GAY uh vihch KRO-OSH chehf*) (1894-1971) was the leader of the Soviet Union from 1958 to 1964. He tried to raise the Soviet standard of living and greatly expanded his country's exploration of space. Khrushchev had little pity for weaker nations and his political enemies. But he sometimes showed a good-natured humor and the simple tastes of his peasant background.

Khrushchev strongly criticized the cruelty of the Soviet dictator Joseph Stalin, who ruled the Soviet Union, mostly by terror, from 1929 to 1953. Khrushchev also worked to avoid war with the Western nations. This policy helped cause a split between the Soviet Union and China and contributed to Khrushchev's fall from power.

Khrushchev was born on April 17, 1894, in Kalinovka, near Kursk, in southwestern Russia. His father was a poor peasant who also worked as a coal miner. In 1918, Nikita joined the *Bolsheviks* (later called Communists), who had seized control of Russia in 1917. In 1922, the Communist government established the Soviet Union. Khrushchev moved to Moscow in 1929 and soon afterward won the praise of leaders of the Communist Party in Moscow. By 1939, Khrushchev had become a member of Stalin's top executive group, called the Politburo. In 1941, during World War II, Germany invaded the Soviet Union and occupied Ukraine, which was then a republic of the Soviet Union. Khrushchev helped organize troops to fight the Germans there and headed the effort to get war-torn Ukrainian farms, coal mines, and steel mills back into production.

In 1949, Khrushchev became a secretary of the Central Committee of the Communist Party. Stalin died in March 1953, and Georgi Malenkov became premier. Six months later, Khrushchev became first secretary of the Communist Party of the country. Nikolai Bulganin (*nih ko LY bul GAH nihn*) (1895-1975) succeeded Malenkov as premier of the Soviet Union in 1955.

In 1956, revolts took place against the Communist governments of Poland and Hungary. Khrushchev sent troops and tanks to crush the uprising in Hungary. On March 27, 1958, he replaced Bulganin as premier of the Soviet Union. Khrushchev became a strong dictator. But he did not rule by terror as Stalin had done, and he reduced the power of the country's feared secret police.

In 1962, Khrushchev threatened the United States by installing missiles on the island nation of Cuba, 90 miles (145 kilometers) south of Key West, Florida. President John F. Kennedy demanded the removal of the missiles, and Khrushchev withdrew them. In October 1964, high officials in the Communist Party forced Khrushchev to retire as both premier of the Soviet Union and first secretary of the party. Khrushchev spent his remaining years writing a book of memoirs called *Khrushchev Remembers,* which was published in English in 1970. He died on Sept. 11, 1971.

In February 1956, Khrushchev called for *peaceful coexistence,* in which the East and West would compete in technological and economic development but avoid war. He also began a campaign of *destalinization* (removal of Stalinist influences) in the Soviet Union and its satellites. In April 1956, the Cominform was dissolved.

Unrest in Eastern Europe

The new Soviet policy led the peoples of Eastern Europe to expect more freedom from Soviet control. In Poland, riots and strikes broke out in June 1956. The rioters demanded a more liberal government and an end to Soviet rule. A few months later, the Soviets allowed Wladyslaw Gomulka (*vlah DIH slahf guh MOO kah*) (1905-1982), a Polish Communist leader, to rejoin the Polish Communist Party. The Soviet Union had jailed Gomulka in 1951 for trying to set up an independent Communist government in Poland. Khrushchev and other Soviet leaders flew to Warsaw to confer with Gomulka in October 1956. Faced with further rebellion, the Soviets agreed to relax some controls in Poland.

Gomulka ended the forced takeover of farmland and eased the campaign against religion. Cardinal Stefan Wyszynski (*vih SHIHN skee*) (1901-1981), the head of the Roman Catholic Church in Poland, was released from prison, and defense minister Konstantin Rokossovsky (*KON stan teen RAW kuh SAWF skee*) (1896-1968), who helped tighten Soviet control in the late 1940's, was dismissed. The Catholic Church would remain a thorn in the side of Poland's Communist government in the coming decades amid further demands for freedom.

In Hungary, a revolt against Communism began in October 1956. Preceding the revolt, unrest grew, especially among writers, young people, and others deeply concerned with human rights and freedom of expression in response to the policies of Matthias Rákosi (1892-1971),

A crowd cheers Hungarian troops in Budapest in 1956. The Hungarian people revolted against their Communist government and Soviet domination. Soviet troops quickly crushed the revolution. But opposition to Communist control continued.

head of the Communist Party and head of the Hungarian government. Rákosi was replaced as party leader in mid-1956, but his policies were continued.

A rebel government led by Imre Nagy (*IHM ray NOJ*) (1896-1958), who had been the head of government from 1953 to 1955 and attempted reforms before being forced out by Rákosi, demanded withdrawal of all Soviet troops. The revolution spread swiftly through Hungary. Many political prisoners were freed, including József Mindszenty (*mihnd ZEHN tih*) (1892-1975), a cardinal and head of the Roman Catholic Church in Hungary who had been jailed by Communists in 1949.

Nagy again became prime minister and declared Hungary to be a neutral country. But the new government lasted only a few days.

Early in November, Soviet tanks rolled into Hungary's capital, Buda-

In July 1956, Egypt seized the Suez Canal, which was owned mainly by the British and French. In October, Israel invaded Egypt. In November, the United Kingdom and France attacked Port Said, Egypt, in an attempt to retake the canal. In this photograph, smoke rises from oil tanks beside the Suez Canal after the Port Said attack.

pest. The fighting spread to all parts of the country. The Soviet Union smashed the revolt in about two weeks. Thousands of Hungarian "freedom fighters" were killed. About 200,000 fled Hungary. Mindszenty took refuge in the United States Legation (now the U.S. Embassy) in Budapest, where he lived until allowed to leave Hungary in 1971. Nagy and his co-workers were charged with helping plot the revolution. They were convicted of treason and were executed in 1958. The Soviet Union would not allow Hungary to break up the bloc of Eastern European satellites, keeping the country under tight Communist control. János Kádár (*YAH nawsh KAH dahr*) (1912-1989), the new head of the Communist Party, served as prime minister from 1956 to 1958 and from 1961 to 1965, following stern policies designed to prevent further revolutionary acts in his first term.

The Suez crisis

As the Soviets dealt with unrest in Eastern Europe, trouble stirred in the Middle East. Both the Soviet Union and the West sought Egypt's support by offering aid for its development plans. Each side offered to help build the Aswan High Dam. After Egypt courted Communist aid for the dam and bought Communist arms, the United States and the United Kingdom canceled offers to help with the project. President Gamal Abdel Nasser (*gah MAHL AHB duhl NAH sehr*) (1918-1970) of Egypt struck back by taking over the Suez Canal from international control. He said Egypt would use profits from operating the canal to build the dam "without pressure from any nation." But he still accepted Soviet aid.

In October 1956, during the Hungarian revolt, Israel invaded Egypt. The United Kingdom and France immediately joined in the attack. They wanted to return the Suez Canal to international control. The United States and the Soviet Union supported a United Nations resolution demanding an immediate truce. In addition, the Soviets threatened to send troops to help Egypt. The UN arranged a truce after a few days of fighting. But by backing Egypt against Israel, the Soviets had won friends among the Arab countries of the Middle East.

The missile gap

Khrushchev's power in the Soviet Union reached its peak in the late 1950's. Sometimes his government followed a hard policy, mainly in response to China's challenge to Soviet leadership of the Communist bloc. At other times, the Soviets stressed peaceful coexistence, giving special attention to economic aid and scientific progress. But the Soviet Union continued to encourage "wars of liberation." As a result, the United States came to regard "peaceful coexistence" as the Communist effort to conquer countries without a major war.

As the Soviet Union improved its ability to produce nuclear weapons, the Western bloc feared a *missile gap*—that is, that Soviet rockets and other weapons would be superior in numbers and power to those of the West. In 1957, the Soviets tested the first intercontinental ballistic missile (ICBM). They also launched the first artificial Earth satellite, Sputnik 1. In January 1958, the United States launched its first Earth satellite. A brief thaw in the Cold War followed. The Soviets stopped testing nuclear weapons in March 1958, and the United States halted its tests in October.

The Eisenhower Doctrine, approved by the U.S. Congress in March 1957, pledged American financial and military aid to Middle East nations that asked for help against Communist aggression. In July 1958, a revolution ended the rule of the pro-Western government of Iraq. Nearby Lebanon feared a Communist revolution and asked the United States for aid. Eisenhower quickly sent sailors and Marines to help Lebanon. The United Kingdom sent paratroopers to protect Jordan against Iraqi pressure.

During the late 1950's, Europe remained the center of the Cold War. In November 1958, the Soviet Union demanded peace treaties for East and West Germany. Such treaties would have ended the military occupation, and Western troops would have had to leave. The United States refused, keeping its forces in Berlin.

Another temporary thaw in the Cold War began in the spring of 1959. The foreign ministers of France, the Soviet Union, the United Kingdom, and the United States met in May. In July, U.S. Vice President Richard M. Nixon visited the Soviet Union and met with Khrushchev. Two months later, Khrushchev visited the United States, meeting with Eisenhower at Camp David in Maryland. Khrushchev was so friendly that observers spoke of the "spirit of Camp David," recalling the earlier "spirit of Geneva." Eisenhower and Khrushchev planned a *summit* (top-level) conference to be held in Paris in 1960. The president accepted Khrushchev's

In July 1959, U.S. Vice President Richard M. Nixon (right, at microphone) visited the Soviet Union and met with Soviet Premier Nikita S. Khrushchev (left, wearing hat).

invitation to visit the Soviet Union after the summit meeting.

The friendly relations between the United States and the Soviet Union would last less than a year before an incident between the two nations caused renewed tensions. On May 1, 1960, an American U-2 spy plane was shot down in Soviet territory. The Soviet Union captured the pilot, Francis Gary Powers (1929-1977), who confessed he was a spy. U.S. President Eisenhower accepted personal responsibility for the flight. He admitted that U-2 planes, which carried cameras, radar, and other

Soviet Premier Nikita S. Khrushchev (second from right),
and his wife (far left), were guests of the U.S. President
Dwight D. Eisenhower and his wife, Mamie, in 1959.
Khrushchev's visit temporarily eased U.S.-Soviet tensions.

On May 1, 1960, a missile strike disabled a U-2 spy plane over the Soviet Union, forcing the pilot to bail out. The captured pilot and the plane's wreckage forced the United States to admit to spying.

sensory equipment, but no weapons, had been taking photographs over the Soviet Union for years. After the Paris conference began on May 15, Soviet leader Khrushchev demanded that Eisenhower apologize for the U-2 incident. Eisenhower refused, and Khrushchev angrily canceled his invitation for the president to visit the Soviet Union. The U-2 incident abruptly ended the 1959 thaw in the Cold War.

Cuban leader Fidel Castro (lower right), watches the fighting during the Bay of Pigs invasion in April 1961. The U.S.-supported invasion failed badly.

CHAPTER FIVE

Crises in Cuba and other JFK Cold War challenges

On July 26, 1953, Fidel Castro (*fih DEHL KAS troh*) (1926-2016), a young lawyer, tried to start a revolution against the government of Cuba led by the corrupt and ruthless dictator Fulgencio Batista y Zaldívar (*fool HEHN syoh bah TEES tah ee sahl DEE vahr*) (1901-1973) by organizing an attack on the Moncada army barracks in Santiago de Cuba. Fidel and his brother Raúl were captured and imprisoned. Many of their followers were either imprisoned or murdered.

In 1957, the rebel forces began to wage a guerrilla war against the Cuban government. (*Guerilla warfare* is warfare conducted by roving bands of fighters who stage ambushes, sudden raids, and other small-scale attacks.) The same year, university students stormed the presidential palace in an attempt to assassinate Batista. Attempts by the government to crush dissent increased the people's support of the rebels. Continued poor economic conditions also led to growing support for the rebels, particularly among workers, peasants, students, and the middle class. By mid-1958, Batista's government had lost the support of the United States and most Cubans.

On Jan. 1, 1959, Batista fled the country. The Castro rebel forces then took control of the government. Fidel Castro became prime minister of Cuba. The new Cuban government quickly set out to change Cuban relations with the United States. In particular, it sought to reduce U.S. influence on Cuban national affairs. In 1959, for example, the Cuban government seized U.S.-owned sugar estates on the island. As a result, U.S.-Cuba relations quickly became strained. As relations with the United States deteriorated, Cuba developed stronger economic ties with the Soviet Union. In 1960, Castro's government signed a broad trade pact with the Soviet Union.

In June 1960, the Castro government took over American and British oil refineries in Cuba after the refineries refused to process crude oil imported from the Soviet Union. The United States then stopped buying sugar from Cuba. Over the next few months, the Castro government took over all the remaining American businesses in Cuba and accepted Soviet offers to purchase Cuban sugar. In October 1960, the United States placed an economic embargo on Cuba, which banned all U.S. exports except medicines and some food products.

In January 1961, the United States ended diplomatic relations with Cuba. That year, the Cuban government led by Castro became increasingly Communist. Castro condemned the United States and began to receive military aid from the Soviet Union and other Communist countries. The Cuban government seized millions of dollars' worth of American property in Cuba.

Bay of Pigs invasion

On April 17, 1961, about 1,400 Cuban exiles sponsored by the United States landed at Playa Girón (*PLAH yuh hee ROHN*) and Playa Larga, two beaches on Cuba's southern coast near the Bay of Pigs [Bahía de Cochinos (*BY ee ah day koh CHEE nohs*)]. The exiles planned to advance into Cuban territory and establish a provisional government. However, the terrain around the landing sites was swampy, which made it difficult for them to establish a *beachhead* (foothold) and move into the countryside.

The invasion ended on April 19, after more than 1,100 members of the exile unit, known as Brigade 2506, were captured. More than 100 members died in battle, and some others escaped to the interior of the island to join anti-Castro guerrilla groups. The Cuban government has never revealed exactly how many Cuban troops died in the invasion. The rebels' defeat led to a widespread crackdown on political opponents of Cuba's government and solidified Castro's control of the country.

Experts have suggested several explanations for the invasion's failure. Before the attack, the U.S. media had reported information about Cuban exile training camps in Guatemala, which compromised the secrecy of the operation. In addition, just two days prior to the invasion, exile pilots flying old bomber planes provided by the U.S. Central Intelligence Agency had failed in an attempt to destroy the Cuban Air Force. Castro's government had arrested many of its opponents in Cuba so that they would not be able to join the attack, and Cuban troops greatly outnumbered the exiles.

Also, historians believe that poor planning and the U.S. government's failure to provide air support for the rebels led to their defeat by Castro's forces. The unsuccessful invasion damaged the reputation of the U.S. government. It is regarded as one of the worst foreign policy blunders of U.S. President John F. Kennedy's administration.

After the exiles' capture, the United States began negotiations with Cuba to secure their release. In December 1962, the Cuban government freed the exiles in return for baby food and medicines worth $53 million.

Cuban missile crisis

In October 1962, the United States learned that the Soviet Union had secretly installed missiles in Cuba, about 90 miles (140 kilometers) from Florida. The missiles could have been used to launch nuclear attacks on American cities. President Kennedy demanded that the Soviets remove

MRBM LAUNCH SITE 2
SAN CRISTOBAL
1 NOVEMBER 1962

FUEL TRAILERS

MISSILE-READY TENT

FORMER LAUNCH POSITIONS

FORMER LOCATION OF MISSILE-READY TENTS

One of the most serious incidents of the Cold War was the Cuban missile crisis of 1962. Communists had come to power in Cuba in 1959. In October 1962, the United States learned that the Soviet Union had installed missiles in Cuba that could launch nuclear attacks on United States cities. The crisis passed after Soviet leader Nikita S. Khrushchev and U.S. President John F. Kennedy agreed that the Soviets would remove their missiles from Cuba in return for the removal of U.S. nuclear missiles from Turkey and Kennedy's promise that the United States would not invade Cuba. Shown here is an aerial photograph of a missile launch site in San Cristobal, Cuba.

the missiles. He also ordered a naval blockade of Cuba to stop further shipment of arms. Navy ships were ordered to turn back ships delivering Soviet missiles to Cuba. Kennedy also called about 14,000 Air Force reservists to active duty.

For a time, it appeared that the United States would invade Cuba to destroy the missiles. At one point, an invasion was scheduled for October 29 or October 30. Experts believed that such an invasion would probably mean war—most likely nuclear war—with the Soviet Union.

After a week of extreme tension, Khrushchev and Kennedy reached an agreement, ending the crisis. Khrushchev ordered all Soviet offensive missiles removed. Kennedy then lifted the blockade.

Kennedy also promised that the United States would not invade Cuba and that it would remove U.S. nuclear missiles from Turkey. Turkey was

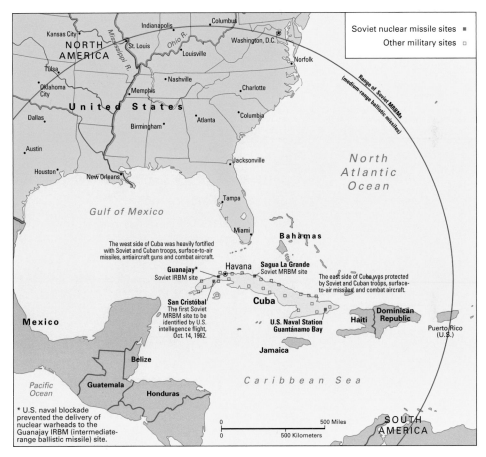

The Cuban missile crisis brought the United States and the Soviet Union to the brink of war. On Oct. 16, 1962, the United States learned that the Soviet Union had installed missiles in Cuba that could launch nuclear attacks on U.S. cities. President John F. Kennedy ordered a naval blockade and planned to invade the island. American and Soviet leaders completed an agreement ending the crisis on October 28.

John Fitzgerald Kennedy

John Fitzgerald Kennedy (1917-1963) was the youngest man ever elected president of the United States, and he was the youngest ever to die in office. He was shot to death on Nov. 22, 1963, after two years and 10 months as chief executive. The world mourned Kennedy's death, and presidents, premiers, and members of royalty walked behind the casket at his funeral. Kennedy was succeeded as president by his vice president, Lyndon B. Johnson (1908-1973).

Kennedy, a Democrat, won the presidency with his "New Frontier" program, after a series of television debates with his Republican opponent, Vice President Richard M. Nixon. At 43, Kennedy was the youngest man ever elected president. (Theodore Roosevelt was 42 when he became president upon the death of William McKinley. He was 46 when he was elected president.) Kennedy was the first president of the Roman Catholic faith. He also was the first president born in the 1900's.

In his inaugural address, President Kennedy declared that "a new generation of Americans" had taken over leadership of the country. He said Americans would "... pay any price, bear any burden, meet any hardship, support any friend, oppose any foe to assure the survival and the success of liberty." He told Americans: "Ask not what your country can do for you—ask what you can do for your country."

On Oct. 7, 1963, U.S. President John F. Kennedy (seated) signed the Limited Nuclear Test Ban Treaty, which prohibited the testing of nuclear weapons under water and on or above ground. The president's signing took place in the Treaty Room at the White House in Washington, D.C.

Kennedy became widely known by his initials, JFK. He won world respect as the leader of the Free World. He greatly increased U.S. prestige in 1962 when he turned aside the threat of an atomic war with the Soviet Union while carrying out negotiations that resulted in the Soviets withdrawing missiles from Communist Cuba.

The Kennedy action marked the start of a period of "thaw" in the Cold War as relations grew friendlier with the Soviet Union. In 1963, the United States, the Soviet Union, and over 100 other countries signed a treaty outlawing the testing of atomic bombs under water and on or above ground. On the home front, the United States enjoyed its greatest prosperity in history. African Americans' campaigns for civil rights still denied them caused serious domestic problems, but African Americans made greater progress in securing equal rights than at any time since the American Civil War (1861-1865). During Kennedy's administration, the United States made its first piloted space flights and prepared to send astronauts to the moon.

a U.S. ally that bordered the Soviet Union. Kennedy agreed privately to dismantle all U.S. missile bases in Turkey. The agreement between Kennedy and Khrushchev regarding the missile bases in Turkey was kept secret because many Americans opposed such a deal. Almost all Americans thought that Kennedy had forced the Soviet Union to remove the missiles from Cuba simply by threatening war. Some experts believe that, as a result, U.S. foreign policy used greater toughness and more threats of force after the crisis.

The Cuban missile crisis was one of the most serious incidents of the Cold War. It brought the United States and the Soviet Union to the brink of war.

Other JFK Cold War challenges

In 1961, the Soviet Union threatened to give Communist East Germany control over the West's air and land supply routes to Berlin. The threat was part of a Soviet effort to end the combined American, British, French, and Soviet control of Berlin, begun in 1945, when World War II ended. The Western nations opposed any threat to the freedom of West Berlin.

In June 1961, Kennedy discussed Berlin with Khrushchev at a two-day meeting in Vienna, Austria. Nothing was settled, and the crisis deepened. Both countries increased their military strength.

In August 1961, amid increasing tensions between the Soviet Union and United States, growing numbers of East Germans fled to West Germany. To stop this flight, the East German Communists built a wall of cement and barbed wire between East and West Berlin. The Berlin Wall was constructed as a system of heavily fortified barriers that was about 26 miles (42 kilometers) long. It included a wall of massive concrete slabs that varied from 12 to 15 feet (3.7 to 4.6 meters) in height. Pipes, barbed wire, and other obstacles were installed on top of much of the wall.

In June 1961, U.S. President John F. Kennedy (right) discussed Berlin with Soviet Premier Nikita S. Khrushchev at a two-day meeting in Vienna, Austria. Earlier that year, the Soviet Union threatened to give Communist East Germany control over the West's air and land supply routes to Berlin.

Kennedy called up about 145,000 members of the National Guard and reservists to strengthen U.S. military defense. They were released about 10 months later.

For the next 28 years, the East Berlin side featured armed guards, guard dogs, barbed wire, electric alarms, mines, and trenches. The Communists also erected walls and other barriers around the rest of West Berlin. The length of the barriers totaled about 110 miles (177 kilometers). In response, the United States sent additional troops and tanks to West Berlin. Some East Germans were able to escape after the wall was built. Others, however, were killed by Communist border guards. More than 170 people died trying to escape from East Germany by crossing over the Berlin Wall. Most of them were shot by border guards.

In 1961, the United States established the Alliance for Progress, a 10-year program of aid for Latin American countries that agreed to begin democratic reforms. Kennedy hoped this program would bring social and political reform as well as fight poverty.

The western Atlantic alliance remained strong, but Kennedy had trouble establishing a united NATO nuclear force. President Charles de Gaulle (1890-1970) refused to commit France to the NATO nuclear force. He preferred an independent role for his country. Kennedy made a 10-day tour of Europe in the summer of 1963. He visited West Germany, Italy, Ireland, and the United Kingdom.

Southeast Asia continued to be a trouble spot. Kennedy ordered U.S. military advisers to the area in 1961 and 1962 when the Communists threatened South Vietnam and Thailand. Kennedy also sent advisers to Laos. In the summer and autumn of 1963, the United States severely criticized the South Vietnamese government headed by Ngo Dinh Diem (*uhng oh dihn zih ehm*) (1901-1963) for its repressive policies against the country's Buddhists. The government imprisoned many Buddhist leaders and students who were leading demonstrations against the Diem government. Kennedy sent former Republican senator and vice presidential candidate Henry Cabot Lodge, Jr., to South Vietnam as ambassador in 1963.

In September 1961, the Soviets resumed testing atomic weapons. The tests broke an unofficial test ban that had lasted nearly three years. The United States began testing shortly after the Soviets resumed their tests, but the United States conducted its tests underground, which created no dangerous fallout. But in April 1962, the United States resumed

The Berlin Wall divided Berlin into Communist East Berlin and non-Communist West Berlin. East Germany, backed by the Soviet Union, built the wall to prevent East Germans from emigrating to the West. This photograph shows East German workers reinforcing the Berlin Wall near the Brandenburg Gate in 1961.

testing in the atmosphere over the Pacific Ocean.

After the missile crisis in Cuba, Cold War tensions again eased. In July 1963, the United States, the Soviet Union, and the United Kingdom approved a treaty to stop the testing of nuclear weapons in the atmosphere, in outer space, and under water. Testing was permitted underground. Many countries that had no atomic weapons also signed the treaty.

In August, the United States and the Soviet Union installed a *hot line,* a direct communications link between the White House and the Kremlin (the Soviet seat of government) to reduce the risk of nuclear war. Also in 1963, Kennedy approved a plan to sell the Soviets $250 million worth of American wheat. The two nations also agreed to cooperate in some space projects. When Kennedy was assassinated on Nov. 22, 1963, Lyndon B. Johnson became president and continued to work for peaceful coexistence with the Soviet Union.

The Saturn 5 rocket launches the Apollo 11 mission from Kennedy Space Center, Florida, on July 16, 1969. The moon race ended on July 20 when American astronauts Neil Armstrong and Buzz Aldrin reached the lunar surface.

CHAPTER SIX

The space race

The Cold War rivalry between the U.S. and U.S.S.R. space programs became known as the "space race," a period of intense competition between the United States and the Soviet Union to achieve supremacy in space exploration. During the Cold War, the threat of nuclear war between the countries motivated them to develop space technology. Neither side wanted to appear too warlike. Space exploration provided competition between the two countries without the stakes of potential war. The United States and the Soviet Union raced to build bigger spaceships, including those that could reach different planets and others to be piloted to the moon.

The space race had its roots in World War II. During the war, Germany had developed relatively simple rockets. It used them to bomb the Netherlands and Great Britain. Following the war, the Soviet Union and the United States recruited German scientists to develop their rocket technology. Both sides quickly started trying to outdo each other by building better rockets that could go great distances.

By 1947, the Soviet Union had secretly begun a massive program to develop long-range military missiles. In the 1940's, the small but influential British Interplanetary Society published accurate plans for piloted lunar landing vehicles, space suits, and orbital rendezvous. A U.S. group, the American Rocket Society, concentrated on missile engineering. In 1950, a new International Astronautical Federation began to hold annual conferences.

In 1955, both the United States and the Soviet Union announced plans to launch artificial satellites with scientific instruments on board. The satellites were to be sent into orbit as part of the International Geophysical Year, a period of international cooperation in scientific research beginning in July 1957. The Soviets provided detailed descriptions of the radio equipment to be included on their satellite. But the Soviet rocket program had been kept secret until that time. As a result, many people in other countries did not believe that the Soviets had the advanced technology required for space exploration.

Sputnik

On Oct. 4, 1957, the Soviets stunned the world by succeeding in their promise—and by doing so ahead of the United States. Only six weeks earlier, the Soviet two-stage R-7 missile had made its first 5,000-mile (8,000-kilometer) flight. This time, it carried Sputnik (later referred to as Sputnik 1), the first artificial satellite. *Sputnik* means *traveling companion* in Russian. The R-7 booster hurled the 184-pound (83-kilogram) satellite and its main rocket stage into orbit around Earth. Radio listeners worldwide picked up Sputnik's characteristic "beep-beep" signal.

The Western world reacted to the launch of Sputnik with surprise, fear, and respect. Soviet Premier Nikita S. Khrushchev ordered massive funding of follow-up projects that would continue to amaze and dazzle the world. A month after Sputnik, another Soviet satellite, Sputnik 2, carried a dog named Laika (*LY kuh*) into space. The flight proved that animals could survive the unknown effects of microgravity. In the United States, leaders vowed to do whatever was needed to catch up. And so the "space race" began.

More Soviet successes followed. In 1959, Luna 2 became the first probe to hit the moon. Later that year, Luna 3 photographed the far side of the

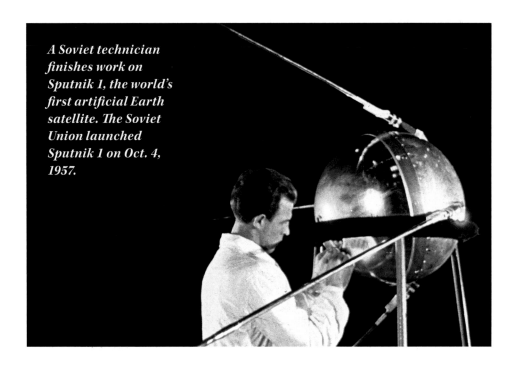

A Soviet technician finishes work on Sputnik 1, the world's first artificial Earth satellite. The Soviet Union launched Sputnik 1 on Oct. 4, 1957.

moon, which cannot be seen from Earth. The third Soviet milestone occurred on April 12, 1961, when cosmonaut Yuri Gagarin (*YOOR ee gah GAHR ihn*) (1934-1968) entered orbit aboard the spacecraft Vostok 1. In doing so, he became the first human space traveler, a few weeks before the United States sent its first astronaut into space.

The first United States satellite was Explorer 1, launched on Jan. 31, 1958. Next was Vanguard 1, which was launched on March 17, 1958. These and later U.S. satellites were much smaller than their Soviet counterparts because the rockets the United States used to carry satellites were smaller and less powerful than those used by the Soviet Union. The Soviet Union's rockets gave it an early lead in the space race. Because bigger rockets would be needed for piloted lunar flight, both the United States and the Soviet Union began major programs of rocket design, construction, and testing.

Soviet cosmonaut Yuri A. Gagarin became the first person in space, on April 12, 1961. Gagarin's Vostok spacecraft completed one orbit of Earth. The flight lasted 108 minutes.

A key to the ultimate success of U.S. space programs was centralized planning. In 1958, a civilian space agency called the National Aeronautics and Space Administration (NASA) was established. NASA absorbed various aviation researchers and military space laboratories. The formation of NASA helped forge agreement among competing interests, including military branches, universities, the aerospace industry, and politicians.

The moon race

In 1958, both the United States and the Soviet Union began to launch probes toward the moon. The first probe to come close to the moon was Luna 1, launched by the Soviet Union on Jan. 2, 1959. It passed within about 3,700 miles (6,000 kilometers) of the moon and went into orbit around the sun. The United States conducted its own lunar fly-by two months later with the probe Pioneer 4. The Soviet Luna 2 probe,

The first seven U.S. astronauts, selected for the Mercury program, are shown here in front of a U.S. Air Force F-106B jet aircraft. They were, from left to right, M. Scott Carpenter, Gordon Cooper, John H. Glenn, Jr., Virgil I. Grissom, Walter M. Schirra, Jr., Alan B. Shepard, Jr., and Donald K. Slayton. The program lasted from 1958 to 1963.

launched on Sept. 12, 1959, was the first probe to hit the moon. One month later, Luna 3 circled behind the moon and photographed its hidden far side.

The Soviet Union began to test lunar hard-landers in 1963. After many failures, they succeeded with Luna 9, launched in January 1966. The U.S. Surveyor program made a series of successful soft landings beginning in 1966. Between 1970 and 1972, three Soviet probes returned lunar soil samples to Earth in small capsules. Two of them sent remote-controlled jeeps called *Lunokhods,* which traveled across the lunar surface.

Beginning in 1966, the United States sent five probes called Lunar Orbiters into orbit to photograph the moon's surface. The Lunar Orbiters revealed the existence of irregular "bumps" of gravity in the moon's gravitational field caused by dense material buried beneath the lunar surface. These areas of tightly packed matter were called *mascons,* which stood for *mass concentrations.* If the mascons had not been discovered, they might have interfered with the Apollo missions that sent astronauts to the moon.

After several delays, the United States sent its first astronaut into space on May 5, 1961. Astronaut Alan B. Shepard, Jr. (1923-1998), flew into space aboard the project Mercury capsule Freedom 7. However, Shepard did not complete an Earth orbit. The first U.S. astronaut to orbit Earth was John H. Glenn, Jr. (1921-2016), on Feb. 20, 1962.

Three months later, astronaut M. Scott Carpenter (1925-2013) repeated Glenn's three-orbit mission. A six-orbit mission by Walter M. Schirra, Jr. (1923-2007), in October 1962 further extended the testing of the space-craft. The final Mercury mission took place in May 1963, with Gordon Cooper (1927-2004) aboard. The mission lasted 1.5 days.

Meanwhile, the Soviet Union continued to launch Vostok missions. In August 1962, Vostok 3 and Vostok 4 lifted off just a day apart and passed near each other in space. Another two capsules—Vostok 5 and Vostok 6—were launched in June 1963. One of the pilots spent almost five days in orbit, a new record. The other pilot, Valentina Tereshkova (*VAH lehn TEE nah teh rehsh KAW vah*) (1937-   ), became the first woman in space.

The U.S. and the Soviet Union launched larger crews for longer flights. The world's first multiperson space capsule, Voskhod (Sunrise)—later referred to as Voskhod 1—was launched on Oct. 12, 1964. Cosmonauts

Astronaut John H. Glenn, Jr., became the first American to orbit Earth. On Feb. 20, 1962, Glenn circled the planet three times in less than five hours. He made his historic flight in a spacecraft named Friendship 7. Glenn resigned from the astronaut program in 1964. From 1974 to 1999, he served as a United States senator from Ohio.

Vladimir M. Komarov (1927-1967), Konstantin P. Feoktistov (*fay OKS tih KOV*) (1926-2009), and Boris B. Yegorov (1937-1994) spent 24 hours in orbit. They became the first space travelers to land inside their capsule on the earth, rather than in the ocean.

In March 1965, cosmonaut Alexei A. Leonov (1934-   ) stepped through an inflatable air lock attached to Voskhod 2 to become the first person to walk in space. After the capsule's automatic flight control system failed, Leonov and Pavel I. Belyayev (*behl YAY ehv*) (1925-1970) had to land it manually on its return to Earth. They missed their planned landing zone and came down in an isolated forest. The cosmonauts had to fend off wolves until rescuers reached them the following day.

The first piloted Gemini mission, Gemini 3, was launched on March 23, 1965. Astronauts Virgil "Gus" Grissom (1926-1967) and John W. Young (1930-   ) used the capsule's maneuvering rockets to alter its path through space. With Gemini 4, launched on June 3, 1965, copilot Edward H. White II (1930-1967) became the first American to walk in space. The astronauts aboard Gemini 5, launched on Aug. 21, 1965, spent almost eight days in space, a record achieved by using fuel cells to generate electricity.

Gemini 6 was originally intended to link up with an Agena rocket sent into space a few hours earlier. After the unpiloted Agena was lost in a booster failure, NASA combined Gemini 6 with an already scheduled 14-day Gemini 7 mission. Gemini 7 was launched as planned, on Dec. 4, 1965, and Gemini 6 took off 11 days later. Within hours, Schirra and Thomas P. Stafford (1930-   ) moved their spacecraft to within 1 foot (30 centimeters) of Gemini 7 and its crew, Frank Borman (1928-   ) and James A. Lovell, Jr. (1928-   ). The two spacecraft orbited Earth together for several hours before separating.

On March 16, 1966, Gemini 8 completed the world's first docking of two space vehicles when it linked up with an Agena rocket in space. However, the spacecraft went into a violent tumble. Astronauts Neil A. Armstrong (1930-2012) and David R. Scott (1932-   ) managed to regain control of the spacecraft and make an emergency splashdown in the western Pacific Ocean.

Additional tests of docking and extravehicular activity took place on the remaining four Gemini missions. On these missions, astronauts and flight controllers also gained vital experience in preparation for the

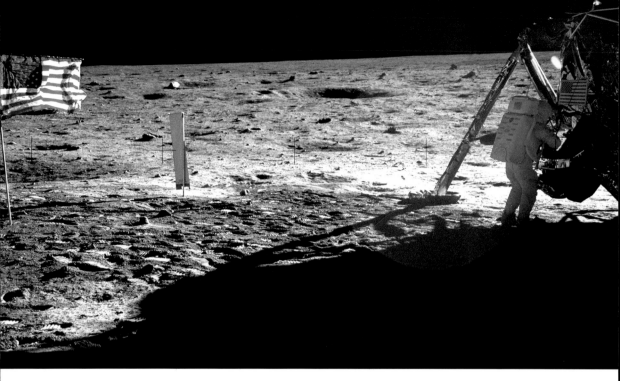

This photograph shows the American astronaut Neil A. Armstrong, commander of the Apollo 11 mission to the moon, working at a storage assembly on the lunar module Eagle. The historic first extravehicular activity (EVA) on the lunar surface, in July 1969, also included the American astronaut Edwin E. "Buzz" Aldrin, Jr., who took this photograph. Most photos from the Apollo 11 mission were taken by Armstrong and show Aldrin. This photograph is one of only a few that show Armstrong.

tremendous challenges of piloted lunar flight.

The United States and the Soviet Union built larger and more advanced satellites. In addition, they sent probes to the moon, Mars, Mercury, and Venus. The Soviet Union launched the first probes aimed at another planet, two Mars probes, in 1960. However, neither probe reached orbit. After more Soviet failures, the United States launched two Mariner probes toward Mars in 1964. Mariner 4 flew past the planet on July 14, 1965, and sent back remarkable photographs and measurements. The probe showed that the atmosphere of Mars was much thinner than expected, and the surface resembled that of the moon.

The Soviet Union launched the first probes toward Venus in 1961, but these attempts failed. The first successful probe to fly past Venus and return data to scientists on Earth was the U.S. Mariner 2, on Dec. 14, 1962. Mariner 5 flew past Venus in 1967 and returned important data. Mariner 10 passed Venus, and then made three passes near Mercury in 1974 and 1975.

On May 25, 1961, U.S. President John F. Kennedy essentially challenged the Soviet Union to a moon race. Kennedy declared it a U.S. goal to put an astronaut on the moon before the decade was over. For a time, the Soviet Union took up the challenge. The Soviets built the N1 moon rocket and a lunar lander. They practiced *docking* (coupling spacecraft together) and other skills needed to land a person on the moon. But the Soviet effort suffered setbacks, including four N1 launch failures. The moon race ended on July 20, 1969, when U.S. Apollo 11 astronauts Neil Armstrong and Buzz Aldrin (1930-   ) reached the lunar surface. The six Apollo moon landings remain the only missions to successfully land humans on the moon. By beating the Soviets to the moon, the U.S. had "won" the space race.

Officials in the Soviet Union publicly denied there had ever been a Soviet equivalent to the Apollo program. This official story became widely accepted around the world. But in the late 1980's, the Soviet Union began to release new information indicating that the Soviet government had an ambitious lunar program that failed.

Soviet plans for piloted lunar flight may have been hampered by a lack of central authority. Rivalry among different spacecraft design teams and other space organizations prevented cooperation. The Soviet equivalent of the Apollo CSM was a two-person lunar modification of the Soyuz capsule, called the L-1. The Soviet lunar module, the L-3, resembled the LM developed in the United States. However, it would carry only one cosmonaut. The Soviet booster, the N-1, was bigger than the Saturn 5 but less powerful, because it used less efficient fuels.

Piloted Soviet L-1 capsules were scheduled to fly past the moon as part of a test program. This program was planned for 1966 and 1967, well before the United States could attempt a lunar landing. The Soviet Union conducted unpiloted test flights under the cover name *Zond*. Three pairs of Soviet cosmonauts trained for a lunar mission.

The Soviet moon ships had serious problems. Many of the boosters for the L-1 lunar fly-by blew up. In addition, the unpiloted L-1 spacecraft developed serious flaws. It was still too dangerous to allow cosmonauts aboard. Soviet efforts to reach the moon were also frustrated by the continued failure of the giant N-1 booster. Four secret test flights were made between 1969 and 1972. However, all of the vehicles exploded.

After the moon landings, the space race eased. Historians often date its end to the joint U.S.-Soviet mission known as the Apollo-Soyuz Test Project. On July 17, 1975, a U.S. Apollo capsule and a Soviet Soyuz capsule linked together in Earth orbit. The Soviet and American crews performed experiments together in space.

Propaganda posters for the Chinese People's Liberation Army sought to stoke fears of major attacks from the West. In this poster, Red Army and Red Guard members charge forward, holding the bible of their movement, Quotations from Chairman Mao *(1964). Mao was the head of the Chinese Communist Party.*

CHAPTER SEVEN

Balance of power

The character of the Cold War changed again in the mid-1960's. The United States and Soviet Union each had large numbers of nuclear weapons. Each had an antimissile defense system. But both powers realized that there would be no victor in an all-out nuclear war. As a result, the two sides sought greater stability and cooperation in their relationship. Also, conflicts within both the Eastern and the Western blocs changed the two-sided nature of the balance of power.

By 1960, the Soviet Union and the Communist People's Republic of China were quarreling bitterly and openly. The Soviet Union cut off technical aid to China. After China attacked India in 1962, the Soviets supported India. The Soviet Union again backed India when Pakistan and India fought in 1965. China threatened India and aided Pakistan.

In 1966, China launched a "cultural revolution" to eliminate all Soviet and Western influence from China. The Chinese accused the Soviet Union of betraying world Communism and secretly allying with the United States. The Chinese threat to the Soviet Union became more serious after China exploded its first hydrogen bomb in 1967. In 1969, a border dispute led to Soviet and Chinese troops fighting on an island in the Ussuri River. This river formed the border between Chinese Manchuria and Soviet Siberia, including Vladivostok, an important port on the Pacific Ocean. The fighting soon ended, but the border controversy remained unsettled.

Some Soviet satellite countries also shifted their loyalties. Albania

Leonid Ilyich Brezhnev

Leonid Ilyich Brezhnev (*LAY oh nihd ihl YEECH BREHZH nyehf*) (1906-1982) headed the Communist Party of the Soviet Union from 1964 until his death. In this position, he became the most powerful leader in the country. Brezhnev greatly increased Soviet military strength but could not solve growing economic problems.

Brezhnev was born on Dec. 19, 1906, in Kamenskoye (*ka MEHN skoy uh*) in southwest Russia (now Dniprodzerzhynsk, Ukraine). He studied surveying and became a land surveyor. He joined the Communist Party in 1931. That year, he entered night school at a metallurgical institute in Kamenskoye. After graduating, he served in the army for a year before becoming a party official and director of a technical school.

During World War II, Brezhnev worked as a political adviser in the Soviet Army. He became allied with Nikita Khrushchev, then a senior Communist Party official. After the war, Brezhnev held several high posts in the Communist Party. After Soviet dictator

Joseph Stalin died in 1953, Khrushchev became head of the Communist Party. As Khrushchev's political fortunes rose, so did Brezhnev's.

In 1957, Brezhnev became a full member of the Presidium, the small group that ran the Communist Party. In October 1964, Brezhnev and other leaders forced Khrushchev to retire. Brezhnev replaced Khrushchev as leader of the Communist Party.

Brezhnev pursued stable relations and increased trade with Western countries, especially the United States. He signed several arms control treaties. At the same time, he greatly increased Soviet military strength, kept tight control over Communist countries in Eastern Europe, and supported revolutionary movements in Asia and Africa.

In 1979, the Soviet Union invaded Afghanistan to support Afghanistan's Communist government against rebel forces. The United States and its allies condemned the invasion and adopted political and economic sanctions against the Soviet Union.

In domestic affairs, Brezhnev maintained the Communist Party dictatorship. The Soviet economy grew weaker in the 1970's. The war in Afghanistan was a failure. After Brezhnev's death on Nov. 10, 1982, Soviet leader Mikhail Gorbachev (*mih kah EEL gawr buh CHAWF*) blamed many of the country's problems on Brezhnev.

In June 1967, Soviet Premier Aleksei Kosygin (second from left) met with U.S. President Lyndon B. Johnson (at podium) in the United States to discuss the Vietnam War, the Arab-Israeli dispute, and arms control.

sided with China in 1961. Yugoslavia remained independent. Josip Tito called for "national Communism"—the idea that each country should achieve Communism in its own way, free of Soviet influence. Other Communist nations, including Romania, Poland, and Cuba, loosened their ties with the Soviet Union.

Differences also sharpened among the Western nations. French President Charles de Gaulle challenged the leadership of the United States and the United Kingdom. France established diplomatic relations with China in 1964. France also criticized U.S. policy in the Vietnam War (1957-1975). At de Gaulle's request, NATO moved its military headquarters from Paris to Brussels, and the French reduced their troop commitment to the alliance. France also blocked the United Kingdom's entry into the European Economic Community (EEC), a forerunner of the European Union. France then sided with the Arabs against U.S.-backed Israel in the 1967 Six-Day War.

The growing strength of Europe was another factor in the changing nature of the Cold War. More than 20 years after the end of World War II, the nations of Western Europe had prospered. The EEC, also called the European Common Market, had become a powerful economic force. Western European nations gradually increased trade with Communist countries.

In 1964, Leonid Ilyich Brezhnev (*LAY oh nihd ihl YEECH BREHZH nyehf*) (1906-1982) and other Soviet Communist Party leaders forced Khrushchev to retire, giving Brezhnev leadership of the party and the Soviet Union. Under Brezhnev's 18-year tenure, the Soviet Union's improved relationship with the United States coincided with a Soviet military buildup.

Soviet-American relations in the 1960's reflected the changing nature of the Cold War. In 1966, the Soviet Union and the United States agreed to permit direct air service between Moscow and New York City. In January 1967, they and 60 other nations signed the first international treaty providing for the peaceful exploration and use of outer space. In June, Soviet Premier Aleksei Kosygin (*ah lehk SAY ko SEE gihn*) (1904-1980) met with President Johnson to discuss the Vietnam War, the Arab-Israeli dispute, and arms control. Kosygin also addressed the UN General Assembly in New York City.

In August 1967, the Soviet Union and the United States began working on a treaty to prevent the spread of nuclear weapons. The treaty also provided for international inspection and controls. The U.S. Senate approved the agreement in 1969. The Treaty on the Non-Proliferation of Nuclear Weapons went into effect on March 5, 1970, after being *ratified* (formally approved) by the Soviet Union, the United Kingdom, the United States, and more than 40 other nations. In 1969, Soviet and U.S. representatives began a series of Strategic Arms Limitation Talks

(SALT) to control the production of nuclear weapons.

Relations with Europe

During the early 1960's, Czechoslovakia's agricultural and industrial production dropped, and there were shortages of food and other goods. Even members of the Communist Party criticized the government's inability to reverse the economic decline. At the same time, the country's intellectuals called for more freedom of expression, and many Slovaks renewed their efforts to gain recognition for Slovak rights. In 1968, the Communists removed Antonín Novotný (*AN TAW neen naw VAWT nee*) (1904-1975) as party leader. Alexander Dubcek (*DOOB chehk*) (1921-1992), a Slovak, became the party leader, and Ludvík Svoboda (*lood VEEK svoh BOH duh*) (1895-1979) became the country's president.

Under Dubcek, the government introduced a program of liberal reforms. These reforms included more freedom of the press and increased contacts with non-Communist countries. Dubcek won popularity among Czechoslovakia's people for the reforms, known as the Prague Spring.

Soviet and Warsaw Pact troops invaded Czechoslovakia in August 1968, since leaders of the Soviet Union and other European Communist nations feared that Dubcek's program would weaken the party's control in Czechoslovakia. The invasion halted the Prague Spring. Soviet troops forced Czechoslovakia to remain a Soviet satellite. The Soviet troops remained, but the other troops withdrew by late 1968. This invasion crushed hopes for an easing of Cold War tensions in Europe.

In April 1969, the Czechoslovak Communist Party replaced Dubcek with Gustáv Husák (*GUS tahv HOO sahk*) (1913-1991), another Slovak Communist. Thousands of people who had been active in the reform movement either resigned or were removed from the party. In 1975, Husák succeeded Svoboda as president while continuing to serve as

Alexander Dubcek (left), a Slovak, became head of the Czechoslovak Communist Party, in 1968. Dubcek won popularity among Czechoslovakia's people for his reforms, known as the Prague Spring.

Communist Party leader. Under Husák, Czechoslovakia remained a tightly controlled Communist state and a loyal ally of the Soviet Union.

Unrest also occurred in Bulgaria in the 1960's. During the early 1960's, the country still suffered from a severe shortage of basic goods and services. In addition, some members of the government began to resent Soviet influence in Bulgaria. In 1965, Todor Zhivkov (*ZHIHV kawv*) (1911-1998), who had become head of state in 1962, survived an attempted military takeover of his government. For the next 20 years, Zhivkov based his rule on sharing power between national and local government authorities, improving living standards, and maintaining close ties with the Soviet Union. He continued policies that restricted the freedom of Bulgaria's people.

Meanwhile, Romania, which had resented Soviet interference since the 1950's, became open to the west. Romania's leaders then began expanding industry and increasing trade with Western nations in the

Czech youths hold Czech flags and stand atop an overturned truck
as other residents surround Soviet tanks in downtown Prague.
Soviet and Warsaw Pact troops invaded Czechoslovakia in August
1968. The invasion halted the Prague Spring.

1960's. Five years after exchanging ambassadors with the United States,
Romania's leaders hosted a visit by U.S. President Richard M. Nixon in
1969. They also declared Romania neutral in a dispute between the
Soviet Union and China. In 1965, Romania adopted a constitution that
called for the nation's complete independence. In 1977, Romania began
strengthening its ties with the nations of the *nonaligned movement*.
These nations, primarily in Asia and Africa, had refused to support
either the Communist or non-Communist bloc.

The Vietnam War

The Vietnam War heated up the Cold War. During the early 1960's, the

United States stepped up its support of South Vietnam against the Communist Viet Cong forces. The United States blamed the struggle on Communist North Vietnam and viewed the conflict as "aggression from the north." However, many Vietnamese saw the conflict as a fight for liberation from foreign domination begun against France and then continued against the United States.

The U.S. military effort gradually increased. Large-scale bombing of North Vietnam began in 1965. By 1968, the United States had over 500,000 troops in Vietnam. The Viet Cong and North Vietnamese received war materials from the Soviet Union and China.

The fighting spread throughout Indochina. Cambodia and Laos, both of which bordered South Vietnam, tried to stay neutral. But Communist forces used both countries as bases for raids into South Vietnam, and the two nations were drawn into the war. Thailand backed the West in the struggle. The United States used bases there for bombing raids on North Vietnam.

In 1969, the United States began reducing its troop numbers while training the South Vietnamese to take over the fighting. In 1973, the United States withdrew the last of its ground forces. Communist troops conquered South Vietnam in 1975, ending the war. Different Communist groups then took power in Cambodia and Laos. The defeat in Vietnam dealt a blow to the reputation of the U.S. government and its military.

While the United States drew down its forces in Vietnam, it joined in multilateral negotiations to address various issues regarding the Cold War. The Helsinki Accords included an agreement that would presage the closing of the Cold War. However, such agreements did not prevent further tension between the United States and the Soviet Union when Afghanistan rose as another "hot" dispute. Also, some Soviet satellites continued their fight for freedom from Soviet control during the 1970's.

YOU ARE LEAVING
THE AMERICAN SECTOR
ВЫ ВЫЕЗЖАЕТЕ ИЗ
АМЕРИКАНСКОГО СЕКТОРА
VOUS SORTEZ
DU SECTEUR AMERICAIN
SIE VERLASSEN DEN AMERIKANISCHEN SEKTOR
U.S. ARMY 5

Checkpoint Charlie was a tightly controlled crossing point at the Berlin Wall between East and West Berlin. This photograph was taken in 1976.

CHAPTER EIGHT

The final act

The loosening of ties among members of both the Communist and Western blocs led to new international relationships in the 1970's. Several Communist and democratic nations developed friendlier relations, helping ease tensions. In 1970, West Germany and Poland signed a treaty to reject the use of force and to recognize the boundaries created in Europe after World War II. West Germany and the Soviet Union ratified a similar treaty in 1972.

The status of West Berlin had long been a major Cold War problem. In 1971, France, the Soviet Union, the United Kingdom, and the United States signed an agreement stating that West Berlin was not part of West Germany. The agreement also allowed free movement of traffic between West Germany and West Berlin. In 1973, after the pact took effect, East and West Germany joined the United Nations.

Also in 1973, the United Kingdom finally entered the economically powerful European Community, as the European Union was then called. At the same time, Japan's prospering economy allowed it to adopt a more independent role in international relations.

China's relations with the West improved in the early 1970's. Canada and several other Western nations established diplomatic relations with Communist China for the first time. China was admitted to the UN in October 1971. In February 1972, U.S. President Richard Nixon met with Chinese Premier Zhou Enlai in China. The two agreed to increase contacts between their two countries. In 1979, the United States and

Strategic Arms Limitations Talks

The Strategic Arms Limitation Talks (SALT), a series of meetings between the Soviet Union and the United States, took place between 1969 and 1979. The two nations met in an attempt to limit the production and distribution of nuclear weapons. United States President Lyndon B. Johnson proposed the talks in January 1967, hoping to end the costly U.S.-Soviet arms race. At that time, the Soviets were trying to overtake the United States in the production of offensive intercontinental ballistic missiles (ICBM's) and submarine-launched missiles. Later, the Soviets began building an antiballistic missile (ABM) system to defend Moscow.

The first round of SALT meetings lasted from 1969 to 1972. The meetings took place in Helsinki, Finland; Vienna, Austria; and Geneva, Switzerland. A second round, held in Geneva, lasted from 1973 to 1979.

The first round of meetings led to two major U.S.-Soviet agreements signed in 1972. The two agreements together became known as SALT I. One agreement was a treaty limiting each country's defensive missile system to two ABM sites with no more than 100 missiles at each site. The treaty was later changed to allow each nation only one site. The other SALT I pact limited distribution of certain offensive nuclear weapons for five years. Both agreements went into effect in 1972.

In 1979, another round of SALT talks led to the signing of a U.S.-Soviet treaty limiting long-range bombers and missiles. But the pact, known as SALT II, did not officially take effect because the U.S. Senate never ratified it. The Senate stopped

U.S. President Gerald R. Ford (seated, left) and Soviet General Secretary Leonid I. Brezhnev (seated, right) sign a joint communiqué following talks on the limitation of strategic offensive arms in Vladivostok in the Soviet Union, in 1974.

considering the treaty in 1980, partly to protest a Soviet invasion of Afghanistan. But limits under SALT II were observed until 1986.

In 1991, the Soviet Union was dissolved, and most of the former Soviet republics formed a loose confederation of independent states. Key members agreed to abide by the ABM Treaty of SALT I.

In 2002, however, the United States withdrew from the ABM Treaty. United States President George W. Bush claimed that the development of an extensive missile defense system was central to the security of the United States.

China established diplomatic relations. As part of the agreement, the United States ended diplomatic ties with Taiwan.

In 1972, Nixon and Soviet leader Leonid I. Brezhnev signed two agreements, together known as SALT (Strategic Arms Limitations Talks) I. SALT limited the production of U.S. and Soviet nuclear weapons. In 1979, a second pact, SALT II, was meant to limit long-range bombers and missiles. But the United States backed away from SALT II after Soviet troops invaded Afghanistan in late 1979 and early 1980.

The Soviet Union delegation to the Conference on Security and Co-operation in Europe meets on July 30, 1975. Shown left to right are Soviet General Secretary Leonid I. Brezhnev, Andrei A. Gromyko, and Konstantin U. Chernenko.

Helsinki Accords

The Helsinki (*HEHL sihng kee* or *hehl SIHNG kee*) Accords consist of several international agreements reached by the Conference on Security and Co-operation in Europe (CSCE) in the 1970's and 1980's. The CSCE is now known as the Organization for Security and Co-operation in Europe. The first and most important of the accords pledged increased cooperation between the nations of Eastern and Western Europe. The chief agreement was signed in Helsinki, Finland, on Aug. 1, 1975, by

Canada, the United States, the Soviet Union, and the 32 other members of the CSCE, almost all of which were European countries.

The official name of the chief agreement is the Final Act of the Conference on Security and Co-operation in Europe. The Final Act covered many issues. But its main goal was to reduce international tensions associated with the Cold War. The act resulted in the Western countries finally recognizing Eastern European boundaries that had been set up after World War II ended in 1945. In addition, all signers promised to respect human rights, including their citizens' freedoms of thought and religion. The signers also agreed to increase economic and cultural cooperation, to protect the rights of journalists, and to encourage educational exchanges.

After the Final Act was signed, each side charged that the other routinely violated its provisions. For example, the Soviet Union claimed that Western governments' support for Soviet Jews who opposed certain Soviet laws violated a provision against one country's interfering in the internal affairs of another. The Western countries claimed that the same provision prohibited the Soviet invasion of Afghanistan in 1979.

The Final Act led to increased popular demand for the exercise of human rights in Eastern Europe and the Soviet Union. This demand became a major cause of the democratic revolutions that brought non-Communist governments to power in many Eastern European nations in 1989 and the early 1990's. The demand also helped bring about the Soviet Communist Party's fall from power in August 1991. These developments contributed to a sharp improvement in Western countries' relations with Eastern European nations—and with the Soviet Union before it broke up in late 1991.

A year after the People's Democratic Party of Afghanistan (PDPA), the country's Communist party, overthrew and killed Afghan Prime Minister Muhammad Daoud Khan (1909-1978), the Soviet Union became concerned that rebels, who called themselves *mujahideen* (*moo JAH huh deen*), or holy warriors of Islam, might defeat the Afghan government forces. On Dec. 25, 1979, the Soviet Union invaded Afghanistan.

Over the next decade, the Soviet Union sent more than 100,000 troops to join the fight against the rebels. The Soviets had far better equipment than their opponents. But the rebels were supplied by countries opposed to the Soviet Union, including the United States and Saudi Arabia. The mujahideen used guerrilla tactics to overcome the Soviet advantage.

Solidarity in Poland; demonstrations in Lithuania

Even before the Helsinki Accords were formulated, the 1970's also saw continued agitation in Soviet satellites for freedom. In Poland, strikes and riots broke out in Gdansk (*guh DAHNSK*) and other cities in 1970, which were the culmination of protests by Polish intellectuals against government limits on freedom of expression and new disputes that erupted between the government and the Roman Catholic Church.

Thousands of Poles demanded better living conditions and economic and political reforms. After days of riots, Gomulka resigned, and Edward Gierek (*GEE rehk*) (1913-2001) became the Communist Party leader.

Gierek's leadership brought better relations between the government and the Catholic Church. Although Poland remained a loyal ally of the Soviet Union, its government took steps during the 1970's to improve relations with non-Communist countries.

After Polish Cardinal Karol Wojtyla (*KAR uhl voy TIH wah*) was elected the new pope of the Roman Catholic Church in 1978, taking the name John Paul II and becoming the first Polish pope (as well as the first non-Italian pope since 1523), he called on Poland's government to allow its people greater freedom.

Lech Wałesa

Lech Wałesa (*lehk vah WEHN sah*) (1943-   ) was president of Poland from 1990 to 1995. Prior to his election, Wałesa had been an important labor leader.

In 1980, Wałesa was chosen as provisional head of Solidarity— an organization composed of about 50 Polish trade unions. His negotiations with Poland's government that year led to the government's recognition of Solidarity. This action marked the first time a Communist country recognized a labor organization that was independent of the country's Communist Party. Wałesa was elected chairman of Solidarity in 1981. The movement faced growing hostility from Poland's Communist Party and the Soviet Union. In December 1981, Poland's government established martial law and suspended Solidarity's activities. Wałesa and hundreds of other union leaders were imprisoned. In October 1982, the government outlawed Solidarity. Wałesa was released in November. The other prisoners were freed over the next several years.

The government ended its ban on Solidarity in 1989. Also in 1989, it allowed elections for a new Parliament. The elections were the freest ones in Poland since the country became a Communist state in 1945. Almost every candidate who was endorsed by Wałesa and Solidarity won a seat in Parliament. After Wałesa was elected president in 1990, he resigned as chairman of Solidarity.

Solidarity supporters march in a May Day demonstration in Poland on May 1, 1985. Solidarity is an organization composed of Polish trade unions.

Poland struggled with high prices and shortages of food and consumer goods. In 1976, Poles rioted after the government announced big increases in food prices. Government leaders then deferred the increases. Economic conditions worsened in the late 1970's.

During the summer of 1980, thousands of workers in Gdansk and other cities went on strike. They demanded higher pay, free trade unions, and political reforms. Communist leaders promised to meet many of the demands. In September, the Central Committee forced Gierek to resign and elected Stanislaw Kania (*KAHN yuh*) (1927-   ) to

In 1972, many Lithuanian students and young workers demonstrated against the Soviet government. In this photo, Lithuanian protesters take to the streets in May 1972.

replace him. In November, the Polish government recognized Solidarity, an organization of free trade unions. This was the first time a Communist country recognized a labor organization that was independent (free) of the Communist Party. Lech Wałesa (*lehk vah WHEN sah*) (1943-   ) headed Solidarity. (He served as Poland's president from 1990 to 1995.)

In 1972, many Lithuanian students and young workers demonstrated against the Soviet government, and several people burned themselves to death in protest. Lithuanians had resisted Soviet rule since the Soviet Union took over in 1944, including guerilla fighting against Soviet troops from 1944 to 1952. The Soviet government sent about 350,000 Lithuanians to labor camps in Siberia for their political beliefs or as punishment for resisting Soviet rule. The Soviets made the practice of many traditional Lithuanian customs difficult. For example, Soviet laws forbade religious instruction, religious publications, and charity work. People who attended church were kept from good educational and employment opportunities. Lithuanians continued to express opposition to Soviet rule, particularly after the mid-1980's, when the leader of the Soviet Union, Mikhail Gorbachev, began calling for more openness in Soviet society.

As people in Lithuania and Poland persisted in their fight for freedom from Soviet rule through the 1980's, they would be followed by rallies in other Soviet satellites for independence. These countries gained inspiration as Gorbachev called for openness and reform.

A couple of years before these reforms, Gorbachev entered agreements with the United States to reduce armaments. This followed renewed tensions, including another arms buildup, between the Soviet Union and the United States, that occurred in the early 1980's.

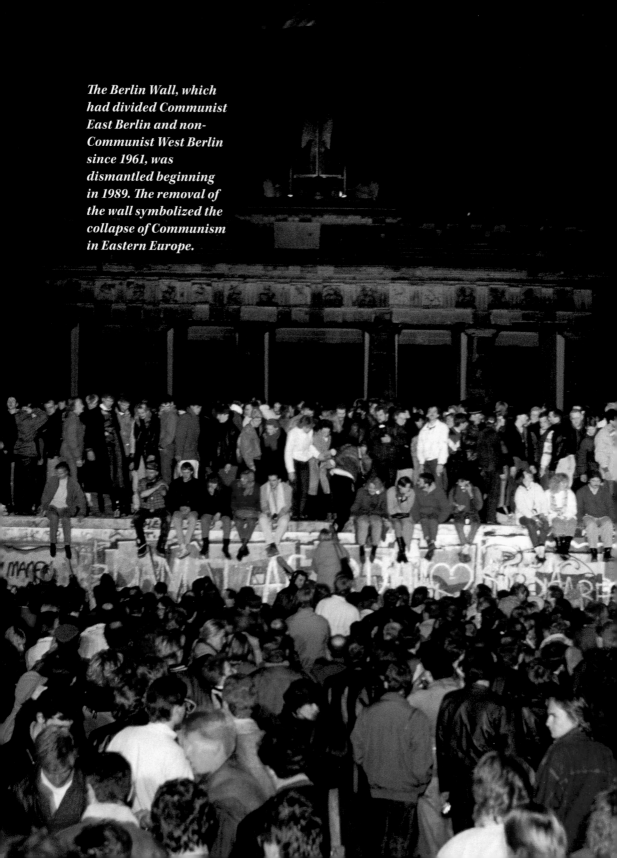

The Berlin Wall, which had divided Communist East Berlin and non-Communist West Berlin since 1961, was dismantled beginning in 1989. The removal of the wall symbolized the collapse of Communism in Eastern Europe.

CHAPTER NINE

The Cold War after 1980 and the breakup of the Soviet Union

Cold War tensions increased in the early 1980's. The renewed friction resulted in part from the Soviet intervention in Afghanistan. It also came from continued American fear of Soviet and Cuban influence in the Middle East, Southeast Asia, Africa, and Central America. United States President Ronald Reagan (1911-2004) and his administration adopted a policy they called *linkage,* tying U.S. arms agreements to the threat of Soviet expansion. (Reagan served as president from 1981 to 1989.)

Meanwhile, the United States, concerned about Soviet military power, increased its defense budget. Critics charged that the build-up was unneeded and too expensive. Reagan insisted that the Soviet Union held a military advantage over the United States. The United States and the Soviet Union held talks to reduce nuclear arms, but they failed to reach an agreement. Reagan then supplied nuclear missiles to U.S. allies in Western Europe. This action further worsened U.S.-Soviet relations.

Also, many observers thought the United States defense build-up would lead to a more dangerous nuclear arms race. But events in the late 1980's led to a sharp reduction in U.S.-Soviet tensions.

In 1987, Reagan and Soviet leader Mikhail Gorbachev signed a treaty to eliminate many nuclear missiles of both nations, including all U.S. and Soviet ground-launched nuclear missiles with ranges of 500 to 5,500 kilometers (310 to 3,420 miles). In 1988 and 1989, Soviet troops withdrew

Afghans cheer as Soviet troops leave Kabul, Afghanistan, on May 15, 1988. That month, Afghanistan, Pakistan, the Soviet Union, and the United States signed agreements providing for an end to foreign intervention in Afghanistan, and the Soviet Union began withdrawing its forces.

Mikhail S. Gorbachev

Mikhail Sergeyevich Gorbachev (*mih kah EEL suhr GAY uh vihch gawr buh CHAWF*) (1931-   ) was the leader of the Soviet Union from 1985 to 1991. As Soviet leader, Gorbachev gained world-wide fame for his efforts to make changes in his country and its relations with other nations. Gorbachev made the Soviet political system more open and democratic, reducing the power of the Communist Party. His call for more openness was known as *glasnost (GLAHS nawst)*. His program of economic and political reform was called *perestroika (pehr uh STROY kuh)* (restructuring). He worked with the United States to decrease the numbers of nuclear weapons. In 1989, Gorbachev withdrew the last Soviet armed forces from Afghanistan. The Soviet military had been involved in Afghanistan since 1979. In 1990, Gorbachev received the Nobel Peace Prize for his contributions to world peace.

Gorbachev was born on March 2, 1931, in the village of Privolnoye, near Stavropol (*STAV roh pohl*). His parents were peasant farmers. Gorbachev joined the Communist Party in 1952. He graduated from Moscow State University in 1955 with a law degree. After graduation, he began a career in the Communist Party organization in Stavropol. He rose through the ranks and became head of the Stavropol regional Communist Party Committee in 1970. He attracted the attention of top Soviet leaders, including Yuri Andropov (*YOO rih ahn DRAWP uhf*) (1914-1984). Gorbachev became a member of the Communist Party's Central Committee in 1971. In 1978, he was brought to Moscow and made party secretary in charge of agriculture.

In 1980, Gorbachev became a full member of the Politburo, the Communist Party's chief policymaking body. Andropov became the head of the party in 1982. He put Gorbachev in charge of economic policy. Andropov died in 1984 and was followed briefly by Konstantin U. Chernenko (*chehr NYEHN koh*) (1911-1985) as party leader. After Chernenko died in March 1985, Gorbachev was chosen party head.

In 1990, the Soviet Union created a new office of president of the Soviet Union. Gorbachev was chosen for this office. The office replaced that of Communist Party head as the country's most powerful position. Gorbachev remained as party head.

In 1991, 13 of the 15 Soviet republics—all except Russia and Kazakhstan—declared independence. On Dec. 25, 1991, Gorbachev resigned as president, and the Soviet Union ceased to exist. He has since remained active in Russian politics.

from Afghanistan.

Also in the late 1980's, the Soviet Union began to reduce its conventional military forces in Eastern Europe. Within the Soviet Union, Gorbachev worked to reduce government control over the country's economic system. He allowed more democracy and freedom of expression in the Soviet Union while encouraging similar actions in Eastern Europe.

U.S. President Ronald Reagan (right) and Soviet leader Mikhail Gorbachev are shown here signing a treaty in 1987 that led to reductions of U.S. and Soviet nuclear arms. Reagan met with Gorbachev several times.

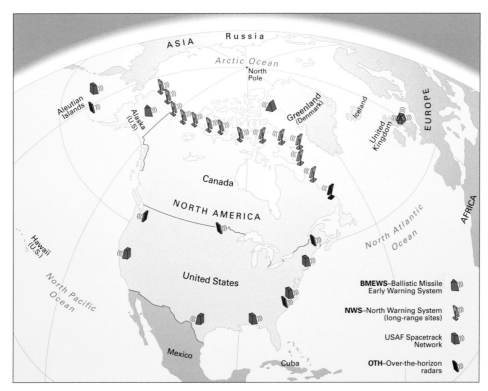

This map shows the locations of various types of radar in North America. Radar is vital to the defense of the United States and Canada. Powerful Ballistic Missile Early Warning System radars warn against long-range missiles. Radars of the North Warning System detect aircraft approaching from the north. Over-the-horizon radars protect against attack from other directions. The United States Air Force (USAF) Spacetrack Network keeps track of artificial satellites orbiting Earth.

The end of Communism in Eastern Europe

Beginning in 1989, Communist rule came to an end in several Eastern European countries, including Poland, Hungary, East Germany, and Czechoslovakia.

The Poles had been persistently fighting for freedom since the 1960's. The Polish government led by Wojciech Jaruzelski (*VOY chehk yah roo ZEHL skee*) (1923-2014) faced continuing economic problems and de-

Ronald Reagan

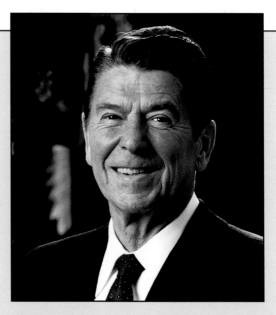

Ronald Wilson Reagan (*RAY guhn*) (1911-2004) was elected president of the United States in 1980 and won a second term in 1984. At the age of 69, he was the oldest man to that time ever elected president. (Donald Trump was 70 upon his election in 2016.) In 1980, Reagan defeated President Jimmy Carter, the Democratic candidate. In 1984, Reagan defeated former Vice President Walter F. Mondale, the Democratic nominee, in a landslide. The president won 525 electoral votes, more than any other presidential candidate in the nation's history. Reagan, a Republican, had served two terms as governor of California before he became president.

Reagan was a skillful campaigner and a gifted speaker. He stressed such traditional values as work, the family, patriotism, and self-reliance. Before Reagan entered politics, he had been an actor nearly 30 years. He appeared in more than 50 movies.

Reagan was born on Feb. 6, 1911, in Tampico, Illinois. He became a sports announcer. On a trip to California, he was hired as an actor.

When Reagan became president, the nation faced serious foreign and domestic problems. Relations between the United States and the Soviet Union had reached their lowest point in years following a Soviet invasion of Afghanistan in late 1979 and early 1980. Reagan strengthened the military systems of the United States and its allies in Western Europe. This angered the Soviet Union. The Reagan administration also increased U.S. involvement in Central America. It gave military equipment to troops fighting Communist-supported forces in El Salvador and Nicaragua. In 1987, Reagan and Soviet leader Mikhail Gorbachev signed a treaty that led to a reduction of certain U.S. and Soviet nuclear arms.

At home, Reagan had to deal with high inflation, a recession, and high unemployment. He won congressional approval of large federal income tax cuts to help stimulate the economy. By the end of Reagan's first term, rapid inflation had ended, unemployment had fallen, and the economy had made a strong recovery. But federal expenses so greatly exceeded income that budget *deficits* (shortages) reached record levels.

In March 1981, a man tried to kill Reagan. The president was wounded but recovered. In the mid-1980's, a U.S. government group secretly and illegally sold weapons to Iran and gave the money to political groups in Nicaragua. Reagan said he knew nothing about these controversial activities.

Reagan wrote two autobiographies: *Where's the Rest of Me?* (1965) and *An American Life* (1990). In 1994, Reagan revealed that he was suffering from the early stages of Alzheimer's disease. The disease causes an increasing loss of memory and other mental processes. He retired from public life. Reagan died on June 5, 2004.

mands by the people for economic improvements and greater political freedom. In December 1981, Jaruzelski imposed martial law. He suspended Solidarity's activities and had Walesa and hundreds of other union leaders held as prisoners. In October 1982, the government officially outlawed Solidarity. Wałesa and some Solidarity members were released in late 1982. The remaining prisoners were released over the next several years. Jaruzelski's government formally ended martial law in July 1983. But many controls over the people's freedom were retained. In 1989, the government reached an agreement with Solidarity that led to the legalization of the union and changes in the structure of the government.

In 1987, Gustáv Husák resigned as Czechoslovakia's Communist Party leader, but remained president. Miloš Jakeš (*MEE losh YAK ehsh*) (1922-   ) succeeded Husák as party leader. In November 1989, hundreds of thousands of people gathered in the streets of Prague (*prahg*), the Czech capital, to demand changes in the government and greater political, economic, and civil freedoms. The demonstrations were followed by general strikes and demonstrations by people across the country. In response to the protests, Communist Party leader Jakeš resigned and Karel Urbánek (*ur BAH nehk*) (1941-   ) replaced him. Also, Czechoslovakia's Communist-controlled Federal Assembly voted to end Communism's leading role in the Czechoslovak government and society.

In December, Marián Calfa (*mah ree AHN CHAHL fuh*) (1946-   ), a liberal Communist, became prime minister and later left the Communist Party. Non-Communists gained control of most key Cabinet ministries. Husák then resigned under pressure. The Federal Assembly elected Václav Havel (*VAH tslahv HAH vehl*) (1936-2011), a non-Communist playwright, to succeed Husák. The end of Communist rule was so

In 1988, Lithuanian intellectuals set up Sajudis, a non-Communist movement to give Lithuania complete control of its economy, citizenship requirements, education, and cultural development. In this photograph, members of Sajudis vote for the independence of the country in Vilnius on October 23.

smooth and peaceful that it became known as the *Velvet Revolution.*

In 1989, Hungary's Communist Party declared that the trial of Imre Nagy and his co-workers and their executions in 1958 had been illegal. Hungary's Supreme Court invalidated the unlawful sentences. Nagy and his co-workers were ceremoniously reburied with honor in June 1989.

Popular power movements were particularly strong in the Baltic republics of Estonia, Latvia, and Lithuania. In 1988, Lithuanian intellectuals set up Sajudis (*SAH yoo dihs*), a non-Communist movement to give Lithuania complete control of its economy, citizenship requirements, education, and cultural development. Sajudis sought to clean up rivers, lakes, and the Baltic Sea shores, all of which had been severely damaged by industrial pollution. Most members of this and similar movements sought total independence and separation from the Soviet Union. Lithuanians supported these goals by staging public demonstrations. They elected supporters of independence as representatives to the Soviet parliament that was created in 1989.

In 1989, Lithuania's parliament expressed a commitment to full independence. It declared that laws adopted by the Soviet parliament were invalid in Lithuania unless approved by the Lithuanian parliament. The government declared Lithuanian the official language. Russian had been the official language under the Soviets. The government also allowed freedom of religion and the press.

On Dec. 7, 1989, the Lithuanian parliament abolished the monopoly of power that the Communist Party had held since 1940, establishing a multiparty political system. Parliamentary elections were held in February 1990. A pro-independence coalition led by Sajudis won over 90 percent of the parliamentary seats.

Through the years, Latvians expressed their national spirit and opposition to Soviet rule. Latvian nationalism became especially strong during the mid-1980's, when Gorbachev began calling for greater openness of expression in the Soviet Union.

In 1988, Latvian reformers established the Popular Front—or People's Front—a large non-Communist organization. The Popular Front sought to gain for Latvia the rights to govern itself and manage its own economy. Most members of the Latvian non-Communist groups sought complete independence from the Soviet Union.

Large numbers of Latvians showed their support for the aims of the Popular Front by holding demonstrations and by electing Popular Front representatives to the Soviet parliament that had been created in 1989. In the late 1980's, the government of the republic agreed to restore the national Latvian flag and anthem, and it began allowing freedom to the press and religious groups. It restored Latvian as the common language. Also, it began lessening government control of the economy. The government began to allow private businesses and farms.

In late December 1989, Latvia's parliament voted to end the Communist Party's monopoly on power. A multiparty political system was established in January 1990. In February, the parliament condemned the Soviet Union's 1940 takeover of Latvia. New parliamentary elections were held in March. Candidates who favored independence from the Soviet Union won a two-thirds majority of the parliamentary seats.

On May 4, 1990, the parliament declared the restoration of Latvian independence and called for a gradual separation from the Soviet Union. The Soviet government called the declaration illegal.

During the late 1980's, a new wave of Estonian nationalism appeared, which was fueled in part by Gorbachev's call for greater openness of expression in the Soviet Union. Most Estonians demanded greater control over their government and economy. Many demanded complete independence from the Soviet Union.

In 1990, Lithuania declared independence, and Estonia and Latvia called for a gradual separation from the Soviet Union. By the end of 1990, all 15 republics had declared that laws passed by their legislatures took precedence over laws passed by the central government.

To prevent further disintegration, Gorbachev proposed a union treaty designed to satisfy demands by the republics for more control over their affairs. In July 1991, Gorbachev and the leaders of 10 republics reached an agreement on a treaty that would give the republics a large amount of independence. The treaty was to be signed by five of the republics on August 20.

The Berlin Wall began to be taken down in November 1989. East Germany reunited with West Germany in 1990. By 1992, nearly all the Berlin Wall had been removed.

Tearing down the wall

East Germany began allowing its people to pass freely to West Berlin through the Berlin Wall in response to demands for more freedom from its residents. The demolition of the wall began in 1989. The opening of the Berlin Wall was hailed as a historic event that symbolized the collapse of Communism in Eastern Europe. East Germany reunited with West Germany in 1990. By 1992, nearly all the Berlin Wall had been removed. Several sections remain standing as memorials, but most of it was broken up for use in roadbeds and other construction projects. Parts of the wall were sold to museums and private individuals.

Soviet control of its Warsaw Pact allies declined sharply in 1989 and 1990. This decline occurred as a result of Communist parties being driven from power in peaceful revolutions in Poland, Hungary, East Germany, and Czechoslovakia. In 1990, Hungary declared that it would no longer participate in military operations associated with the Warsaw Pact and announced its intention to withdraw from the pact by the end of 1991. Poland and Czechoslovakia announced plans to withdraw from the pact as well. In addition, East Germany's membership in the pact ended in 1990, when it became part of a united Germany. In 1991, the leaders of the remaining nations formally agreed to dissolve the pact.

In 1991, the Soviet Communist Party lost control of the Soviet government. On August 19, before the union treaty could be signed, conservative officials of the Communist Party staged a *coup* (attempted overthrow) against Gorbachev's government. The coup leaders imprisoned Gorbachev and his family in their vacation home. The president of the Russian republic, Boris N. Yeltsin (*buh RYEES YEHLT sihn*) (1931-2007), led opposition to the coup, which collapsed on August 21. Yeltsin's role in defying the coup increased his power and prestige both at home and abroad.

After the coup, Gorbachev returned to the office of president, but never regained full power. He then resigned as head of the Communist Party. Also, the Supreme Soviet suspended all Communist Party activities for an indefinite period.

Later that year, the Soviet Union dissolved, and the republics that made up the country became independent states. Russia was by far the largest of these states. The collapse of the coup renewed demands by the republics for a greater amount of control over their own affairs. By November, 13 of the 15 republics—all except Russia and Kazakhstan— had declared independence. However, 11 of the republics—all but the Baltic republics and Georgia—had agreed to remain part of a new, loose confederation of self-governing states. Many of the republics viewed this

Leaders of the 11 ex-Soviet republics who belong to the Commonwealth of Independent States meet on Dec. 30, 1991, to reach an agreement on the military situation in the Soviet Union.

confederation as only a temporary arrangement.

The Congress of People's Deputies formed a *transitional* (temporary) government that would maintain the unity of the country until a new union treaty could be written. The transitional government recognized the independence of the Baltic republics in September 1991.

The final blow to Soviet unity came in December. On December 8, Yeltsin and the presidents of Belarus and Ukraine met in Minsk, Belarus. The leaders announced that they had formed a new, loose confederation called the Commonwealth of Independent States (CIS). They declared that the Soviet Union had ceased to exist and invited the remaining republics to join the commonwealth. Most soon did. The members of the CIS are Armenia, Azerbaijan, Belarus, Kazakhstan, Kyrgyzstan, Moldova, Russia, Tajikistan, Ukraine, and Uzbekistan. Turkmenistan is an associate member.

The CIS was created for several reasons. The economies of the former republics were closely linked, and most members wanted to keep some of those economic ties. Each member also wanted to guarantee its own territory and sovereignty. The members also sought to reassure the rest of the world that the nuclear weapons of the former Soviet Union were under reliable control. Basically, the CIS was intended to help the new countries continue working together and thus make the breakup of the Soviet Union as peaceful as possible.

On December 25, Gorbachev resigned as Soviet president, and the Soviet Union was formally dissolved. In 1993, 12 leaders of the 1991 failed coup against Gorbachev went on trial. The Russian government had charged them with treason and plotting to seize power. In February 1994, the Russian parliament granted amnesty to the coup leaders and freed them.

In 1992, Russian President Boris Yeltsin and U.S. President George H. W. Bush (1946-   ) formally declared that their countries did not regard each other as potential enemies. These events marked the end of the Cold War.

INDEX

FIND OUT MORE!

Books:

Allen, John. *Cause and Effect: The Cold War.* ReferencePoint, 2018.

Fink, Carole K. *Cold War: An International History. 2nd ed.* Routledge, 2017.

Westad, Odd A. *The Cold War: A World History.* Basic Bks., 2017.

Websites:

National Archives: The Cold War. https://www.archives.gov/research/foreign-policy/cold-war

ACKNOWLEDGMENTS

Cover:	NASA; © Daily Herald/Mirrorpix/Getty Images; © Sovfoto/Getty Images; © Hulton-Deutsch Collection/Getty Images
4	© Everett Historical/Shutterstock
6	National Archives
9	WORLD BOOK map
10-11	© TASS/Getty Images
13-15	National Archives
16	ACME News Photo
18	© Bettmann/Getty Images
21	© Tony Linck, The LIFE Picture Collection/Getty Images
22	WORLD BOOK map
24	© AFP/Getty Images
27	WORLD BOOK map
28	Digital Library of Slovenia
30-31	U.S. Air Force
33-34	National Archives
37	University of California, Los Angeles (licensed under CC BY 4.0)
41	Federal Bureau of Investigation
42	National Archives
44	National Nuclear Security Administration/Nevada Field Office
47	Library of Congress
48	WORLD BOOK map
49	© Howard Sochurek, The LIFE Picture Collection/Getty Images
51	© Hulton-Deutsch Collection/Getty Images
52	Public Domain
55	Fortepan (licensed under CC BY-SA 3.0)
56	Public Domain (Fleet Air Arm/Imperial War Museum)
59	Library of Congress
60-61	Dwight D. Eisenhower Library; National Archives
62	© CP Photo/AP Photo
66-69	National Archives
67	WORLD BOOK map
71	John F. Kennedy Presidential Library and Museum
73	National Archives
74	NASA
77	© Sovfoto/Getty Images
78-83	NASA
86	Chinese People's Liberation Army
88	Public Domain
90	Lyndon Baines Johnson Presidential Library
93	Public Domain (Nationaal Archief)
94	© Libor Hajsky, CTK/AP Photo
96	© Ralph Gatti, AFP/Getty Images
99	Gerald R. Ford Library
100-101	© Sovfoto/UIG/Getty Images
104-105	© David Fowler, Shutterstock; © Francois Lochon, The LIFE Images Collection/Getty Images
106	Lithuanian Special Archives
108	© Pool CHUTE DU MUR BERLIN/Gamma-Rapho/Getty Images
110-111	© Robert Nickelsberg, Liaison/Getty Images
112	Vladimir Vyatkin, RIA Novosti archive (licensed under CC-BY-SA 3.0)
114	Bill Fitz-Patrick, The White House
115	WORLD BOOK map
116	Ronald Reagan Library
119	© Pierre Glachant, AFP/Getty Images
122	© Patrick Piel, Gamma-Rapho/Getty Images
124	© Dima Tanin, AFP/Getty Images

...g wakker
...war en
... dier hij
...el? Een vos?
...d misschien?